MONEY

Personal Financial Literacy

For High School Students

Teacher Edition

BY

Debra P. Avara

ISBN-13: 978-1976144288

ISBN-10: 1976144280

Copyright © 2020 by Debra P. Avara

All rights reserved. No part of this book may be reproduced, stored, or transmitted by any means - whether auditory, graphic, mechanical, or electronic - without written permission of both publisher and author, except in the case of brief excerpts used in critical articles and reviews. Unauthorized reproduction of any part of this work is illegal and is punishable by law.

Contents

Introduction..7

Chapter 1: Compound Interest 9

Chapter 2: Individual Retirement Accounts 18

Chapter 3: 401(k) Plan and Transfers 28

Chapter 4: Budgets 38

Chapter 5: Credit and Debit Cards 50

Chapter 6: Paychecks and W2s...............................62

Chapter 7: Income Tax..69

Chapter 8: College and Financial Aid...................77

Chapter 9: Buying a Car...86

Chapter 10: House Buying and Mortgages...........97

Chapter 11: Insurance and Wills.........................110

Answers..118

Appendix...128

Introduction

Money, Personal Financial Literacy for High School Students was written for maximum participation of student involvement. Chapters should be assigned as homework with a discussion taking place in the classroom. Some of the chapters have worksheets or answers to be filled in during class or as homework. Many of the assignments however, will be individual to the student and there will be no set answer. The Answer section of this book will show the worksheets that contain exact answers for grading.

Personal financial literacy is a required topic in high school, earning the student either half a credit or one full credit.

Each chapter will have a list of learning objectives. Teachers should assign chapters as homework with class time used for discussion, clarification and review of the homework as needed.

The Appendix contains the list of standards that this book addresses.

Chapter 1 - Compound Interest

Learning Objectives: At the completion of this chapter, the student is expected to:
1. Analyze types of savings options involving simple and compound interest.
2. Compare relative advantages of these options.
3. Demonstrate an understanding of the importance of saving early and at a sufficient level. to achieve financial security in retirement.
4. Be able to demonstrate the impact of compound growth over time.

Chapter One

COMPOUND INTEREST
HOW IT WORKS

Learning about compounding interest is going to be one of the most exciting moments of your life!! This chapter is going to show you how to make a million dollars, or more, by the time you retire! In this chapter, you will learn how it works, and why you need to know about it NOW! Time, in this instance, is mandatory. The more you have of it (time) the better off you are going to be by the time you retire.

Yes, you heard me right. Retire. You do want to retire someday don't you? Well, without enough money saved, you won't. You will be working for the rest of your life. Not that that is a bad thing, but I would prefer it to be by choice, not a necessity. At this point, let me address a few of the comments running around in your head.

Social Security. You are either thinking, "I will live on my social security" or you are thinking, "There will be no social security by the time I retire." Either way, social security is not enough, in my opinion, to live on comfortably. Yes, you can live on it, but how do you want to live in retirement?

My mom lives on her social security. She has a small house that is paid for, a car that is paid for, and travels some, if she's careful with what she spends. She has a tiny pension she gets every month, but her total income for the month is under $1000. If her house wasn't paid for, or she had a car payment, could she make it? I don't think so.

Personally, I want to be able to travel. I love to travel. And I would like a few "big boy" toys, like jet skis, or a ski boat. I would like to live near the water someday. Can I do that on social security? Nope. Doubt it. So I need to make additional plans for my retirement. If you are in the group that is thinking there won't be any social security, let me just say that I too, have been hearing that since I was a little kid. So, for over 50 years, "there will be no social security when you retire!" Yes, we hear all the time that it won't survive in its current condition, but I think they will change it to fix it. They (being the legislature) have to, there are too many baby boomers coming of age that will be requiring the monthly payment. And, just so you know, the social security that you currently pay out of your pay check goes to the government to help make the current payments to the elderly. So when you are older, the young ones working will be paying in to social security to help make the payments to you. See how it works?

Next myth to address. "I will worry about it later, I'm young, I have plenty of time." NO! You need to be aware of it NOW, and do something about it NOW! NOT LATER. The younger you are when you get started saving for retirement, the more you will have when you retire. So, how many millions would you like to? One? Two? Four? (yes, I'm talking legally!!)

Disclaimer: This is how compounding works. I make no guarantee that you will be able to have the totals listed when you retire. The market fluctuates, and done correctly, you can use compound interest to your advantage.

How It Works

Let's take a look at how compounding interest works. Say you put $1000 into an account that earns 10% interest. How much interest do you earn for the first year? 10% x 1000 = $100. Add that to your original amount and you have $1100.

You don't add any money to your account, but you still get 10% interest. How much do you earn the second year? 10% x 1100 = $110. Add that in (1100 + 110) and now you have $1210. One more time. 3rd year. 10% x 1210 = $121. Add that in to your previous total of $1210 + 121 = $1331.

In 3 years' time, your $1000 has turned into $1331. You earned $331 in interest for just leaving your money in the account. Not bad huh?

Let's look at it this way:

```
1000              1100              1210
x .10             x .10             x .10
 100 + 1000        110 + 1100        121 + 1210 = $1331.
```

$100 + 110 + 121 = $331 interest in 3 years. That may not sound like a lot of money, but if you left that $1000 in the same 10% account for 35 years, you would have $28,102.44.

Now, that amount should have your interest. And yes, I said 35 years. If you work from 30 to 65 years old, that gives you 35 years of savings. If you add 10 years to that savings time frame, from age 20 to 65, you have 45 years of compounding interest time you can work with. In 45 years, your little $1000 will have grown to $72,890.48. If $28K didn't catch your eye, $72K should have!!

This is why I said you need to know this NOW. Get rid of the thinking "I'm too young to worry about retirement. I have plenty of time to worry about that later." Sure, go ahead and wait. But by the calculations above, you see what 10 years of waiting is going to do to you.

EXAMPLE #1

I read an article once that said if you opened an account with $1000, then added $1000 to it for the next 10 years, and you started at age 19, you would make your last $1000 deposit at age 30. Assuming a 12% interest bearing account, you would have $1 million by the time you retired. I thought, "No way, who are they kidding?" I deposit a total of $11,000 over an 11 year time and it's going to grow to over $1million. So I got curious and started playing around with compound interest calculators (found on the internet) and sure enough, they were telling the truth.

Take a look:

　　Current Principal　　$1000.
　　Annual addition　　　1000
　　Years to grow　　　　10
　　Interest Rate　　　　12%
　　Compounded 1 time annually
　　Future value　　　　**$22,760.43**

Now, take that $22,760.43, and leave it in the same account for the next 35 years (age 30 to 65) and it grows the same way your $1000 in the first example did – and you end up with a grand total of **$1,201,742.05**. Nearly $1.25 million. Just for being wise about your money when you are young.

How sweet is that? To have your $11,000 turn into nearly $1.25 million. This is why I say you must learn this NOW. You need to be aware and start saving NOW for retirement if you want one, two, four million dollars by the time you retire.

Ok. So One million dollars is easy. How would you like 2 or 4 million? 8? $8 million. Can you imagine? What would you do with $8 million when you retire? I won't have it because I didn't start early enough. I didn't LEARN about this when I was young. This is one of those hind-site moments YOU don't have to have. Hind-site is always 20-20. If I only knew then, what I know now.

I have one more caveat to make this even sweeter. In the next chapter, I will explain to you how ALL of those millions could be **tax free** to you. That's right; I dare you to read that again. **Tax free**. That means you withdraw the money, and it is NOT taxable to you. But that is in the next chapter. Right now, let's look at what it would take to make more than one million for retirement.

EXAMPLE #2

For this example, let's just open an account, deposit $1000, and then put $1000 into it for 45 years (age 20 to 65). Assuming a 12% interest rate, your grand total would be **$1,685,205.24**.
For your $46,000, ($1000 opening + 45 years of $1000 deposits) you end up with over $1.6 million dollars.

Interest rates are critical for these calculations. The higher they are the better off you are. You may be thinking that 12% is unrealistic. But it really isn't. In my first book, written before the most recent recession, the stock market has historically produced an average of 12%. Unfortunately, this recession was bad enough to lower that 12% to 10%. There are still accounts out there where you can find 12%, but now it's just a bit harder. You do need to pay attention to your money. We will discuss this further in a later chapter. Suffice to say, that if you are very cautious (safe), you will earn less. The higher the interest earned, the higher the risk. I've actually seen some funds that are over 25%, obviously, very, very risky. But looking for and expecting a 10% average, I think is do-able with some work on your part. We'll look at 10%, 11% and 12%, just so you totally get how the interest rate is really important.

Also, let me say here, that you will NOT find these interest rates in a bank. You will need to keep learning, use an online broker and get into a mutual fund, bond fund, something other than a traditional savings account found in banks. More on this later. Let's look at another example:

EXAMPLE #3

Let's look at what that $1000 would do if you saved the same $46,000 over 45 years, but earn 10% interest. Your total would be $863,685.80 -- about 1/2 the amount you receive at 12%. That is why interest rate is critical. But, you know, more than three quarters of a million dollars for your $46K. Still not bad!!

EXAMPLE #4

Let's look at saving $2000 a year. That's only $166.67 a month. That's do-able isn't it? (We'll talk about that in a minute).

For this example, save $2000 a year for that same 19 to 35 age time frame. So you open an account with $2000, and then put $2000 in that account for the next 10 years. How much have you put in? How much is your money? 2000 + (2000 x 10) = $22,000.

For a 12% interest rate, your money would grow to $45,520.86. Then remember, we let it sit for 35 years till we retire at 65. That $45,520.86, just left in that account, grows to **$2,403,484.09.** Woo hoo!! Nearly **$2.5 MILLION** just for saving $22,000 when YOUR WERE YOUNG!!! Not bad, Huh?

This is why you CANNOT wait till your older to start saving for retirement. Well, you can, but you will not reap all the rewards!! And why shouldn't you take advantage of this legal way to get rich. Does it get any easier than this? And all you have to do is save $167 a month. That is just too easy!!

EXAMPLE #5

Look at the exact same example above, with a 10% interest rate. Your $2000 over the first 11 years, would reach $40,249.82.

Leave that money alone for the next 35 years, at 10% interest, and you will have **$1,131,118.02.** That's right!! We are still over ONE MILLION DOLLARS!!

So even if you cannot get that 12% interest, 10% will still get you over the One million dollar mark!! YAHHOOO!! I LOVE IT!! DON'T YOU??

EXAMPLE #6

By now, you get the importance of the interest rate.

For this example, let's save $2000 from age 20 to 65, 45 years total. You open an account with $2000, add $90,000 more ($2000 x 45 years) = $92,000 of your money saved.

At 12% interest, you will have a total of **$3,370,410.48.**

At 11% interest, you will have a total of **$2,409,398.09.**

At 10% interest, you will have a total of **$1,727,371.61. (**Nearly ½ of the 12%, but still not too tacky for only $92K!)

DO YOU WANT MORE?? It really is this easy folks!!

(I actually had a student call me a liar. He didn't believe me. He said, "If it is this easy, why isn't everyone doing it?" I asked him "Did you know about it?" He said no. Bingo. That's why. If you don't know about it, how can you do it?)

EXAMPLE #7

In a future Chapter, I will tell you about Roth IRA's. Currently, you are allowed to save $5500 a year (more if you're older than age 50) for your IRA. Let's look at what saving $5500 a year will do for you. So, we open an account for $5500, and save $5500 for the next 45 years (age 20 – 65).

At 12% interest, you will have (are you sitting down?) a total of **$9,268,628.82.**

At 11% interest, you will have **$ 6,625,844.73.**

At 10% interest, you will have (and you should be sitting for this one too!) a total of **$ 4,750,271.92.**

Even at 8%, you'd have **$ 2,471,405.84**. Still not a shabby number!

And by the way, if you were to put this amount in a regular savings account, *maybe* you'd find 1.5% interest rate, your total would be $332,613.13 – so you can see it's really important to find a fund you like and invest there.

How much of those totals are from your deposits? 5500 + (5500 x 45) = $253,000. $253,000 saved over a lifetime will yield you **MILLIONS** of dollars. How sweet is this?

EXAMPLE #8

I keep telling you that you cannot afford to wait to start saving. If you started saving that $5500 when you reached age 40 (instead of 20), you would only have 25 years to build the interest.

At 10%, your $137,500 (5500 X 25 years) would only yield you **$654,590.59,** a little more than half a million dollars. Eugh. Half a million compared to $4 million plus? Nope, wish I knew this when I was younger.

At 12%, you will have **$ 914,836.99.** That's like 1/10 of the money you would have had if you had started when you were young.

Saving and Investing in YOUR Future

This is pretty exciting, isn't it? But now reality sets in and you are wondering where you are going to scrape up the money to save for your future. Saving $5500 a year breaks down to $459.00 a month (rounded up). That is about $115 a week.

I realize that you may not be able to save $5500 a year right off the bat, but you probably could come up with the $167.00 a month for the $2000 a year. That's only $42.00 a week (rounded up), less than $10 a day, if you have a 5 day work week. Right? $10 is probably near one hour of work per day, to end up with millions when you retire. That would be worth it, wouldn't it?

If you make minimum wage, you might need to save 1 1/2 hours of wages a day. I realize that that may be tough for a while. But surely, as you get older, as you earn more money, you could save more. Now, if you think "I don't have a spare dime to save" – think about what you spend your money on. Do you go to Starbucks? How much coffee do you drink? Out to eat all the time, couldn't you give up one of those? What if you have dessert when you get home? How much does that save?

Do you meet your friends several times a week for appetizers? Meet at some ones' house instead! If they kid you about it, say, "Well, I'm going to be rich when I retire!"

How about starting to buy on sale? Or give up one shirt a month? (If you have expensive taste). Late check fees? Or over-drawn on your checking account fees? Become responsible and pay on time with money you have! Look at all the money you could be saving there!!

Do you read a lot? Use the library! Put your city taxes to good use! Books are free to rent! (Just return them on time!) I love to read, and wasted so much money on books. Now, I use the library. After all, what do we do with those books? Put them on the shelf and then a garage sale for oh, one dollar, when I paid $15? Not a good return for the money.

Do you smoke? How much are you paying a week for cigarettes? My students, here in Texas, just told me the average pack of cigarettes was $6.25. If you smoke one pack a day, your annual cost would be $2281.25. Wouldn't you rather have **$8,000,000.00** instead of black lungs?

Ok, you get the picture! Oh, speaking of pictures, do you go to the movies every week? What are you paying for that? Won't give that up? Do you buy popcorn or soda? Now we are talking serious money! How about renting a movie and popping popcorn at home with a six pack of soda?

You can find *some* money to start saving. Maybe not $5000 a year, but surely, while you are still in school, or before that big raise, you can find some money to start saving for your future.

Financial experts will tell you "pay yourself first." That means you want the most you can have don't you? you save for emergencies and save for retirement, right off the top. Take 10% of your paycheck and save it. You'll be surprised how easy that is when you make it a habit. Have a direct deposit so you don't get tempted to spend the money - out of sight, out of mind. You can do it. After all, you're looking at NOT working someday, and

For you to be financially successful, you need to keep learning, keep asking questions, and keep reading. One publication I get monthly is Kiplinger's Personal Finance Magazine. A year subscription is only about $15.00. It's written so the average person can understand it – mostly. I would encourage you to get a subscription, keep reading, keep learning and pay attention to what they say. They also, nearly monthly, list mutual funds, stock funds, bond funds, etc., how they are performing, what they cost, what their return has been and you can use that to make some decisions on where to invest down the road. <u>Read the articles</u>. Kiplinger's consistently likes three of the online brokers, Fidelity, T. Rowe Price and Vanguard, and they would be a good place for you to start. They are all very helpful and will be glad to help you get started.

Now, one more time, you will NOT find those interest rates in a bank and this money is NOT guaranteed. The market will fluctuate. I've had several students say, "I called every bank in town and none of them have those interest rates." That is correct. They don't. A bank is a good place to start a savings account so you can save up $2000 or whatever amount you need to get started, and then use that money to go to an online broker. You HAVE to use a broker and get into some type of mutual fund to find those interest rates. Again, keep learning. That's what it's all about!

I had a man tell me when I was 18 years old, "Making money is easy. Everyone does it. Keeping it is the hard part." I have never forgotten that, because it is true.

HAPPY SAVING!!

Many of life's failures are people who did not realize how close they were to success when they gave up.
~ Thomas Edison

Chapter 2 & 3 - Roth IRA and 401k

Learning Objectives: At the completion of this chapter, the student is expected to:

1. Understands the implementation of a saving and investing plan.
2. Investigate and compare investment options, including stocks, bonds, certificates of deposit, and retirement plans.
3. Develop a long-term investing strategy to achieve a goal such as a financially secure retirement.

The student uses mathematical processes and is expected to:

1. Discuss the role of financial institutions and markets in saving and investing;
2. Evaluate the costs and benefits of various savings options such as bank savings accounts, certificates of deposit, and money market mutual funds; and
3. Evaluate risk and return of various investment options, including stocks, bonds, and mutual funds.

Chapter Two

Individual Retirement Accounts – IRA's

Once upon a time, there was only one type of IRA. Now that there are two types, they usually refer to the old type as traditional or regular IRA. The 'new' IRA, is the Roth IRA, which I will address next.

Traditional IRA's

IRA's were introduced in 1974 with the enactment of the Employee Retirement Income Security Act (ERISA). Congress originally intended that participants could contribute up to $1,500 a year and reduce their taxable income by the amount of their contributions. Initially, ERISA restricted IRAs to employees who were not covered by a qualified employment-based retirement plan.

This changed in 1981 when the Economic Recovery Tax Act allowed all taxpayers under the age of 70½ to contribute to an IRA, regardless of their coverage under a qualified plan. It also raised the maximum annual contribution to $2,000 and allowed participants to contribute $250 on behalf of a nonworking spouse. The Tax Reform Act of 1986 reversed the trend toward expanded participation by phasing out the deduction for IRA contributions among higher-earning workers who are covered by an employment-based retirement plan themselves or who have a covered spouse. This may sound confusing, but essentially, if you were covered at work, and you made too much money, you could not deduct your contribution from your taxes.

Being able to deduct your contribution from your income was a huge draw for many taxpayers. Congress wanted us to save more for retirement, and they needed to make it attractive. In the 'adjustment to income' section of an IRS 1040 form, we would deduct our contribution which meant we paid less tax. Line 32 of the front of a 1040 is where for 2010, you would deduct your IRA contribution.

In 2002, they raised the contribution to $3000. In 2005, the contribution was raised to $4000. And for 2019, contribution was upped again to $6000 for those who qualified. Phase out amounts – if you made too much money you could not deduct the whole amount - were in place depending on if you were married, how much you made and if you were covered by your employer. And…if you were over 50 years old, you could play catch up along the way by contributing an extra $1000 to your account.

The traditional IRA continued to get complicated by the tax consequences when you contributed (now), and later, when you retired and you take out your money. IF you deducted it now, it was fully taxable later, along with the interest it earned as it grew. IF you could NOT deduct it now, YOU had to keep track of it and NOT pay tax on it later, but the interest it earned was still taxable. The range went from fully taxable now to fully taxable later, and everything in between from partial deduct, partial taxable, etc., etc., etc. Very confusing.

Roth IRA

In 1990, Congress created the Roth IRA, named after Senator Roth who proposed the new IRA. Still trying to entice workers to save for retirement, the Roth IRA had non-deductible contributions, and tax-free withdrawals. There was no question of can I deduct this off my taxes or not? Will it be taxable now or later? Is it a partial deduction? Just plain and simple: you don't deduct your contribution, you pay tax on it now, and when you retire, your withdrawals are tax free. That makes sense.

Did you catch the second part of the Roth IRA? Tax-free withdrawals. When you retire and take your money out to live on, you will NOT be paying taxes on it. That's the good news, the BEST news as far as I'm concerned. Your money is going to grow over the years (remember the compounding interest calculator) and when you start taking it out it is tax free. Yup. You heard me right. **TAX FREE**!! Can you imagine? All those MILLIONS of dollars you saved and invested and you get ALL that interest tax free. That means, just in case you don't get it yet, that you get to WITHDRAW your money for retirement AND NOT PAY TAX ON IT!! FREE, FREE, FREE!! I don't know how it could get better than that.

The contribution amounts are the same as the regular or traditional IRA. You can contribute up to $6000 per year, with the extra $1000 make up when you reach age 50. There *are* limits as to how much you can make in order to still contribute the full amount. For single taxpayers, making more than 114,000/year; and for married filing joint taxpayers making more than $181,000/year, your contribution may be limited as to how much you can put in. (There are back doors to saving your money when you are earning more than that. You can deposit the money in to a Traditional IRA, then roll the amount over to your Roth IRA. Do some quick research when you are earning that much money!!)

The other caveat to these rules is if you make too little!! You can contribute *up to* $6000 per year IF you *make* $6000. If you only make $3000, you can only contribute $3000. Ditto with $1800. If you make $1800, you can contribute $1800. And if you make $7500, you are limited to $6000. Get it? But along with that, as long as you *have* a job, you can start a Roth IRA. You can be 12, mowing lawns for the summer, and contribute the amount you earn for the summer to a Roth IRA account.

There are no age limits – just employment limits. Now, this gets a little tricky with the IRS. If you are self-employed and make over $400 you are supposed to file a tax return. Many of the investment brokers that you might go to to open a Roth IRA, will not deal with someone under the legal age, 18. But there *are* a few out there and you just have to find them. So if you make $350 and want to open a Roth IRA, you can. But you can only contribute $350.

When you turn 15 or 16 and start getting that W-2, you can easily start a Roth IRA. Again, remember that compounding interest calculator and how much you are going to make in interest the earlier you start. Also, the money that goes into the account does not have to be the money *you* specifically earned. In other words, that $350 you earned mowing lawns does not have to be the *same* $350 that goes into the account. If you have birthday money, or your parents or grandparents are willing to help, they can give you all the money or some of the money to send in, just as long as it is not more than $350. If you do start an account before you start getting W-2's, keep a little notebook to keep up with the income you make in case a question ever comes up.

So, the bottom line: If you want to be rich when you retire, you will need to start saving as soon as possible.

This retirement savings is for later. Not for now, not for fun, not for emergencies. You need to have separate accounts set up for emergencies, fun, and big purchases. I, personally, prefer separate accounts for those three things, that way the money doesn't get confused. If I need $3,000 for a trip, and I have $10,000 in an account, then I think I have the money available. When reality is that I saved that $10,000 for emergencies, not for a trip. And emergency money is a must, must, must!!! You never know when you are going to need something in an emergency. This could include just needing a new tire that you hadn't budgeted for.

When we contribute to our retirement fund, we need to consider it gone money. We will 'find' it when we retire. If we don't do this now, when we are younger, when we can, we will not HAVE it later. You MUST sacrifice *some* now, in order to ensure you will have it for retirement. Once you get into the habit of saving some of your income for retirement, and you live within your means, then it is easy. NOT saving for retirement is NOT an option.

How much you need for retirement is up to you. If you want to be able to travel and live a comfortable life, you will need more than someone who does not want or like to travel. If you want to live near a ski slope or on the ocean, you will probably need even more than the person who wants to travel! The life style you want when you retire will determine how much you need to save. And you've already seen by compounding interest calculations that the early you start ….the better!!

Remember, just start saving. You may not have $5500 a year you can save or even $1000. But start with $25 a paycheck, or $50 a paycheck. If you start low, and adjust your budget accordingly, you will be surprised how you can get along without that money. Work your way up and someday you will be saving that $5500 a year!!

Also remember, that when you open your Roth IRA, you can refer back to the compound interest chapter to see how your money will grow. A bank is a great place to *start* a savings account, but once you have a couple of thousand saved up, move it to an online broker. You WILL NOT get the interest rates mentioned in the compound chapter in a bank. You MUST get your money into one of the online brokers to have a chance at those interest rates.

This is a lot of information coming to you. It really is just the basics. But with the basics, you do have enough information to start a Roth IRA. Where to invest your money, who to open a Roth IRA with is your next step. I personally recommend *Kiplinger's Personal Finance Magazine* as a great starting point. It is easy reading and easy to understand. You will find a wealth of information regarding where to invest your money, which their favorite online brokers are, which stocks and mutual funds they recommend to buy, and to sell. An annual subscription is a very affordable $15/year. I recommend this magazine to ALL people and I give several gift subscriptions to family members!!

How To Get Started

Fidelity, Vanguard and T. Rowe Price consistently rank as Kiplinger's most liked online brokers. Whether you want to use them or one of the other online brokers is your choice. Once you have a couple of thousand saved up, *and* you are working, then you are ready to open a Roth IRA. Many brokers have accounts that you can start with $1000 or less.). Go online, find their 1-800 number and give them a call. Tell them that you are brand new to investing and they will be more than happy to help you. Whichever broker you decide to use, they will be very willing to walk you through all the steps to open an account and tell you how to send the money from the bank to them. You will need access to a computer while you are doing this.

One of the newest and easiest funds to buy is the Target Funds. They may be called different things, like Target 2040, or Retirement 2040, but most of the brokerage firms have them now. The year attached is your target retirement year. You do NOT have to buy the one that corresponds to your retirement date. You can buy any of them that you wish, so if one is averaging more than another, feel free to invest in that one. These funds are set up so that the farther from that target date, the more aggressive it will be, earning a higher interest rate. As you get closer to the target date, the brokerage company will transfer – or move – the funds into less aggressive funds, reducing the risk of losing it if/when we hit another slump.

You don't have to do anything other than invest in it and keep sending them money to fund it. You can send money monthly, or annually, or when you have extra. You do not have to be locked into a set amount every month unless you choose that. They'll even do a direct debit out of your checking or savings account on a monthly basis, your choice. Be aware, most do not want to take less than $50 in each deposit. So do check and see what their minimum deposit is. And that's it! You now have your first mutual fund and you are setting up for your future! Congratulations!!

Another area that I want you to be aware of is the fees that the online brokers charge to manage the funds for the year, the expense ratio. Of course you're going to pay *something* for them to manage the mutual fund or bond fund or whatever you invest in. But personally, I won't invest in a fund that charges more than 1% a year. Why? Well, simply because there are plenty of them that are good that charge less than 1%, and, that little bit of fee will really add up over the lifetime that you own the fund. For instance, the difference between a 1% fee and a .9% fee on an account that is worth $10,000 is only $10.00. When that account is worth $100,000, then that fee is $100. Over 30 years, that fee adds up to $5,546 (based on the fund earning 8% annually). That's a lot of money! So watch the expense ratios on the funds you invest in. Also be sure that your fund is a 'no load' fund. That simply means that when you invest in the fund, you don't have to pay extra for them to take your money. You will buy it, you will pay the expense ratio, but you won't pay more – either when you put it in or take it out. So just be careful. Knowing a few of these terms will help you be a wiser investor!

Don't stop learning. You may want to move your fund around, buy something you like better, or stay more aggressive than that fund would allow. The trick is to keep learning and just start saving for your future!

Certificate of Deposit (CD)

A Certificate of Deposit (CD) is a certificate issued by a bank/credit union to a person depositing money for a specified length of time.

A CD is different than a regular savings account. First, there are many options as to how much you have to 'buy'. You can buy a CD for many different denominations ranging from $100 up to $250,000, which is the recommended cap for any single CD because it's also the FDIC insurance limit. Second, you agree or 'commit', to leaving your money in this account for the stated period, which can range from 1 month to up to 5 years, or more, depending on your bank.

Withdrawing your CD early will result in penalties that will affect the total interest you will earn. Each bank is different, so you just have to check.

Many people chose to save their money in CDs because it pays more than a traditional savings account. However, your money is tied up and you don't have access to it in an emergency without paying the penalty of losing a substantial amount of the interest you would have earned upon maturity.

The average regular savings account in 2017 is only .06%. Some banks are paying as little as .01%. Some on line savings accounts are paying up to 1.2%. Some of the online banks have restrictions or requirements in order to earn that rate, so be sure you understand those completely.

In researching CD rates, I found one paying 1.4% with a $2,000 cd for 1 year. However, this same bank is one that is also paying up to 1.2% for their online savings account, without the 1 year requirement. I also found .6% to 2.3% for a cd of $500, but ranging from 6 months to 6 years. Additionally, I found a 3 months to 10 year CD, with a minimum deposit of $2500, ranging from .35% to 2.35%.

Yes, these rates are greater than your regular savings account, but really not much more than the online savings accounts. If you decide to invest in CDs, you must be sure you understand that your money is tied up and you will incur a penalty if you need to withdraw your money early. With that in mind, are you really making any more interest than a good savings account?

Annuity

An annuity is a contract between you and an insurance company that requires the insurer to make payments to you, either immediately or in the future. You buy an annuity by making either a single lump-sum payment or a series of payments. Similarly, your payout may come either as one lump-sum payment or as a series of payments over time typically when you retire.

People may buy an annuity for:

1. Tax deferred interest growth, you pay on the gain when you withdraw the money. (Then why not have a Roth IRA where your interest earned is tax free when you withdraw it?)
2. Death Benefits: If you die before you start receiving payments, your beneficiary gets the money. (Why not just have a term life insurance policy?)
3. Periodic payments for the rest of your life. (Again, you can get this from a Roth IRA.)

There are fixed, variable and indexed annuity's which are all regulated by the state insurance commission and may vary by state. Be sure you understand how these work.

A few of the downsides to an annuity is that you are buying an insurance policy from people that are making a great commission on what they sell you. They are not required to keep your best interest at heart. There are many, many fees that get charged against your annuity. This means it is costing you money every year just to hold it. Annuities are complicated. You are tying up a huge chunk of money for an extended period of time, for potentially a low rate return. Your taxes may also be affected depending on how you take your annuity and what tax bracket you are in.

In my humble opinion, and those of several financial advisors, I would never buy an annuity. Why not just start early with a Roth IRA, invest for your retirement, the interest you earn is tax free when you withdraw it, and you can certainly set it for a distribution based on your life expectancy! And there is only one fee a year that you will be paying. (This fee is just one of the four potential fees you would also be charged with an annuity.) All IRA's have a fee that they charge for them to handle your money. More about that in the Roth IRA chapter.

Happy retirement days!!

A successful man is one who can lay a firm foundation with bricks that others throw at him.
~ David Brinkley

Chapter 1 & 2 Worksheets

Compound Interest and IRA's

Let's play a little bit with a compound interest calculator:
Go to http://www.moneychimp.com/calculator/compound_interest_calculator.htm

Exercise 1:

Plug in these numbers:

Current principal $1000

Annual addition $1000

Years to grow   10

Interest rate   8%

Hit 'Calculate'

    A. What is the answer? $_____

Change the years to grow to 45

    B. What is the answer? $_____

Change the Amounts to $2000 and $2000, with 10 years to grow.

    C. What is the answer? $_____

Change the years to grow to 45.

    D. What is the answer? $_____

Exercise 2:

Take your answer from C. Plug that number into the Current Principal line.

Leave annual edition blank, years to grow 35, interest rate 8% and hit 'calculate'.

    E. What is the answer? $_____

    F. How much of E is the original money YOU put in? _____

    (2,000+ (2k x 10 years) =

Exercise 3:

Start all over but change the interest from 8% to 10%, using $1000 for A & B, and $2000 for C & D.

What do you get for:

    A. $_____

    B. $_____

    C. $_____

D. $_____

Exercise 4:

Go to www.fidelity.com, OR www.vanguard.com OR www.troweprice.com .Look around in the site. You probably will need to play around, but in their 'search' box, type in Target Date Funds.
(https://fundresearch.fidelity.com/mutual-funds/category-performance-annual-total-returns/FREE
(link given for ease in finding Fidelity's list)

Look under mutual funds, or IRA'S and just keep searching around. If you really can't find it, give them a call and ask them how to get to it. Or use their search box for 'target date funds'.

Fidelity calls them VIP Investor Freedom funds.
Vanguard calls them Target Retirement funds.
T Rowe Price calls them Retirement (date ie: 2045) Funds.

(I use these 3 online brokerage firms because Kiplingers Personal Finance Magazine consistently 'likes' these 3 firms.)

What year do you expect to retire? _____
Is there a fund for that year? _____
What is the latest date fund? (ie: 2040, 2045?) _____
Look at the other target date funds. Which one is currently paying the highest interest?
_____

What is the maximum amount you could you invest annually in a Roth IRA if you had the funds?
$_____ (The answer to this is in the chapter, or google it).

Keep in mind, you do NOT have to buy the target date fund that matches your retirement date. You can invest in any of the funds you choose, and move it when you feel the need.

- Call (or go online) your bank or credit union; ask them what their interest rate for a Roth IRA is. What is it? _____

- Would you make more money with an online broker or a bank/credit union? _____
- When should you start saving for retirement? _____

Chapter Three

401(k) PLAN AND TRANSFERS

A 401(k) is a retirement savings plan that allows the employee (you) to save for retirement, and at the same time, save on your current tax liability. The money that you choose to save in your plan, comes out of your paycheck pre-tax (before taxes are taken), and is invested for you in an account, that you may or may not have a lot to say about.

With that said, I have not found a single financial counselor/advisor that says you should not take advantage of the 401(k) plan offered by your employer, if they match at all. IF your employer offers a 401(k) plan, you SHOULD be participating in it. And by now in this book, you understand that the earlier you start saving the better off you are going to be for your retirement years.

401(k) plans used to be easy. You, as the employee, contributes a portion of your wages and the boss, employer, matches a portion of the money you are contributing. So we are talking about FREE money that you are getting from your boss going toward your retirement. That is still the basic concept, and that is still why financial advisors will tell you to participate in your 401(k) plan at work.

And just to be clear, if you do NOT participate in your plan, obviously your boss does NOT make any contributions for you either. You must participate and contribute to your plan if you want your boss to contribute also.

Let's talk about a few of the caveats here: (a caveat is a warning or a caution)

First: Not ALL employers participate in a retirement plan for their employees. So you may indeed have a job that doesn't have a plan. Ok, you can't win them all. There are other ways you can save for retirement.

Second: Not ALL retirement plans are called 401(k). There are 403(b) and 457(b); just depending on the type of employer you have (state government, federal government, corporation, etc). And if you are self-employed, that's another whole ball game that I'm not getting in to! But be aware that there IS a plan for self-employed persons (it's called an SEP).

Third: Making a contribution can take the form of a set dollar amount (take out $20.00) or a percentage (take out 3%) a paycheck. Your employer will also have a <u>maximum</u> amount in percentage form that you can deduct. If your employer only allows 10% of your paycheck, then you are limited to whatever that 10% is going to be, regardless of the amount the IRS says is the maximum. If your employer has a 15% maximum, or even a 20% maximum, again, you may be limited by that % rather than the IRS limits – which brings me to….

Forth: The IRS has limitations on how much you can actually save every year. For 2020, a regular employee can save <u>up to</u> $19,500 per year. If you are over 50 years of age, you can save up to $26,000 per year. The difference in amounts is for 'catch up' and allows the older folk to save more while they think about retirement. However, you are still limited to the *% of your pay that is set by your employer*. Say you make $50,000 a year and your employer limits your contribution to 10%, you can only save $5,000, not $19,500. If your employer allows 15%, then you can save up to $7500.

If on the other hand, you make $180,000 and your boss allows you to save 11%, then you will hit the IRS limit of $19,500 per year. But if your boss allows 15% here, you are still limited to the $19,500. If I'm not mistaken, however, there are further limits involved for high income earners, so be aware that when you are making big, big bucks, you will need to do more research!

Fifth: The amount of matching contribution from your employer will differ. You may have an employer who doesn't contribute any money toward your pension (having the plan is strictly your benefit) – so 0%. Or, your employer may contribute 3% or 6% and I've heard as high as 8%. And yes, even if your employer doesn't match any amount, then you should still participate in the 401(k) plan at work. The tax consequences can still be worth it. Recently, however, I have heard some financial advisors say if they don't match something, then you should invest in a Roth IRA first. If you already max out your Roth IRA, then go ahead and stick with the 401(k) for the tax purposes.

So let's break this down into examples. If you are earning $20,000, and you save 15% of your paycheck, and your boss will contribute 5%, you would be saving $3000 a year and your boss would be contributing $1000 ($20,000 x 5% (NOT 3,000 x 5%)).

Another example: If you are earning $50,000 a year and you're saving 15% you would be saving $7500 a year ($625 a month) toward retirement. If your boss will match 5%, then your boss is throwing in $2500 a year for your retirement. That's free money from the boss.

Your boss may also offer to match 50% *up to* a certain percent, let's say 6% for this example. So if we stick to the same $50,000 example, you may be saving 15% = $7500 a year toward retirement. If your boss will match 50% of 6% (6% of 50,000 = $3000) then your boss is throwing in 50% of $3000 – or $1500.

Sixth: The word 'vested' will probably come into play. What this means is that when you start a 401(k) at your place of employment, your employer will start putting his portion into the account when you do. However, if you *leave* that job for another, before you are 'vested', you do NOT get to take your employers share of the money with you. The vested time is anywhere from 3 months to a year (maybe longer, but I've never heard of it being past a year). You get to take your money, but not your employers. So be sure and check for when you will be vested.

TAX CONSEQUENCE

Now, with some of that out of the way, the next topic is the tax consequences of your 401(k) contributions. When you contribute to your plan, the money comes out pretax. That means before the federal income taxes are withheld from your paycheck, this money comes out and goes into the retirement savings plan. The taxes on THAT money, the money you are saving for retirement, is deferred, you pay it later. You are NOT paying income tax on this money now. If you are earning around $50,000 and saving around $3,000 a year, then you are saving about $750 a year on your income taxes. That's a good thing and another good reason to save for retirement now, you pay less tax.

By the way, Social Security and Medicare taxes will also be withheld from your paychecks total earning, not after your 401(k) is withheld. Not a thing you can do about that, those taxes are not deferred, only income tax is deferred.

Ok, so the thinking behind this is that when you are younger, you will make your most money, being paid the higher salary, which might mean a higher tax bracket. So if we can save money now for retirement, it will lower our income tax bill now – which is assumed to be higher because you are younger and are making more money now, get it? You will pay on this saved money later – hence it becomes a deferred tax consequence. When you retire, and start taking out this money, *then* you pay the taxes on it. But, since your income is lower (usually) when you retire, then your tax bracket will be lower, hence your tax bill will also be lower. See? There is a method to the madness!

Now, wrap your brain around the fact that if you've got a separate Roth IRA (and I certainly hope that you will!) that it is going to be tax FREE, FREE, FREE when you take it out and combine it with the taxes you will pay on this plan, it's a pretty good balance. And yes, you can have both. Do not make the mistake of thinking you can only have one or the other, you can and you SHOULD have both! Just watch out for those income limitations that fall into play when you are making big bucks!

TRANSFERS FROM ONE JOB TO ANOTHER

The biggest mistake I saw people make when I prepared taxes (years ago) was to take out their 401(k) when they left one job for another. Most of the time, they just didn't understand what was happening. Now, you will have no excuse.

Yes, you usually need to take your money with you, or transfer it, but there is a smart way to do it that will not cost you part of the money you already saved. Remember, this money is your future, don't waste it, and certainly don't do anything that allows the IRS to end up with a chunk of it.

Typically, when you go to get your last paycheck, depending on the size of the company, they may try to hand you a check for your 401(k) also, or they say they will mail it to your home. DON'T take that check if it is made out to you. They may insist you take it, they may say you have to take it; they may be real butts about it (I've heard stories). But stand your ground. Say no to them and tell them you will make arrangements.

The law does say you have 60 days to roll your pension over into a *qualified retirement plan*. Yes, that is correct and that's what they may tell you. BUT, and this is a huge *BUT*, when YOU get your hands on that check with your name on it, they are, by law, required to withhold 20% of the money for taxes. 20% of *your* money is going to Uncle Sam. Remember, this money was tax deferred while you saved it. Now that you are getting the money, you need to pay the taxes on it and the IRS wants their share.

So stay with me – If you had $10,000 in your account, the check they hand you will only be $8,000, because they hold out that 20% - 10% for your income tax and 10% for early withdrawal penalty. Now don't jump up and down yet. I can hear you saying, "But I'm not taking it out early by choice, they are making me do it." Well, the IRS doesn't care that you are changing jobs. They don't care that you plan on rolling it over within the 60 days. They want their money now, and if you DO roll it over in 60 days, then they'll give it back to you. But this is where it gets really messy.

Ok - Now you have a check for $8,000 that you can roll over. What about the $2,000 that the IRS has? You would have to take $2,000 out of your *own* pocket to make up the difference so you have a *total* rollover of $10,000. Then you have a ton of icky tricky paperwork to do when it is tax time to get your $2,000 back from the IRS, *IF* you have a preparer that knows what they are doing. So, you might ask, how do I roll it all over without the IRS getting their hands on that chunk of change? Good question, glad you asked! Its way easier than you might think.

Ok, so remember a few paragraphs back I said to tell the people in payroll you will make arrangements? Tell them you will have your new account person get it for you. If you already have an investment account somewhere, like you already have your Roth IRA or a mutual fund with someone, Fidelity, T. Rowe Price, Vanguard, whoever, any of them can do it for you. If you have an account with one of these places, simply call them or get on line and say, "Hey, I've got a 401(k) that needs to be rolled into a 'qualified retirement' plan." They are going to be happy to set it up for you and go get your money for you. THEY are going to get your money – which means YOU are not getting your hands on that check. Hence, Trustee to Trustee, from your old job to the new account. When you do NOT get your hands on that money, they do NOT have to take out that 20% for the IRS. When you go trustee to trustee, the full $10,000 will roll right over for you. Easy breezy, a few signatures and you're done. And truly, any of the online brokers will be more than happy to help you and it can be done *very* quickly. A matter of days, and if you are in an even bigger hurry, fax the paperwork too and from.

If you do NOT have an account with one of the brokers and don't have time to choose one quickly, run down to your local bank and tell them the same thing. Set up a 'qualified retirement' plan at your local bank and they will go get your money for you. All done electronically, very quickly, and the full $10,000 will be rolled over. Once it's transferred, you have time to find an investment broker you want to set up with. No, I would NOT leave it in a bank, you will get a better interest rate with one of the investment brokers. Then, do the exact same thing. Set up an account with an investment broker and say the same thing "I have a qualified retirement plan sitting in X Bank that I need rolled over to you." And they are going to be happy to do it for you.

When it comes to doing your income taxes, your 1099R will be (should be) marked appropriately as a complete rollover and no problems. No icky tricky paperwork trying to be sure your taxes are filled out properly for you to get your money back from the IRS, because with trustee to trustee, it was never taken out! Now, isn't that good news?? Much easier going trustee to trustee – and you still have the full amount in your retirement account that will continue to grow for your future.

My son recently changed jobs. His last job had a 401(k) plan that he had a little bit of money in. He received a letter from the employer asking him how he wanted to handle his money. Did he just want a check or do a rollover? He chose the rollover and filled out the paperwork. They didn't, however, ask for his account number, or give instructions to have the new trustee go get the money. I was confused as to how his money was going to get to the new account, so I called the people where the money would go and asked about it. They said one of the new ways to do it now was that the old employer would send my son the check, made out to the new people, not in his name. He would get it, put the account number on it and mail it in. A few days later my son received a phone call from the 'old' trustee and asked him again if it was going to be a rollover into a regular IRA or a Roth IRA. Since it was going to a Roth IRA, they reminded him that he would have to pay taxes on this now. Remember, 401(k)s are tax deferred now, whereas Roth IRA deposits are not tax deferred. You have already paid on the money you choose to deposit to your Roth IRA now, not later when you withdraw it like a 401(k). They offered to hold out the 20% for the taxes, but reminded him that once he made the rollover, he would have to make up that 20% in order for it to be a 100% rollover. (Hang in there, I know this is confusing). Since the amount was not very much, about $350, he chose to just get the whole amount, no taxes withheld, and he would pay the taxes at tax season. And, since this was going to be a rollover, they said ok to not withholding the taxes, as long as he knew he would still have to pay them. Now, I'm not sure if they would have still agreed to not withholding the taxes if the amount was more than it was, since it was going to a Roth IRA. But in this case, they did. If we had said a 'qualified retirement plan' or a traditional IRA, taxes would not have been an issue. *And*, we might have chosen a 'qualified plan' if the amount was larger than it was (so he wouldn't have to pay taxes on the rollover), and if the amount was larger, would it have gone from trustee to trustee??

All of this may sound very confusing, there is a lot going on. While my son was talking to these people, he was on speaker phone with me beside him telling him yes, no, ask this, etc. etc. When we were finished, he said "What just happened?" I explained it quickly, and I think he understood most of it. The point of me telling you this is that it is difficult to understand. Both the old employer and the new broker people were very nice and answered all the questions and explained things fully. If we had more questions, or if you have questions, they will help you. My point is to tell you to ask those questions!

Beware – when preparing your tax return, make sure you look it over carefully. Make sure that you do NOT have your rollover sitting in the taxable income section of your 1040, and that there is not an early withdrawal penalty tax in the tax section. If you do, then the 1099R was NOT coded properly in the computer tax program and it needs to be corrected. Or, your preparer missed a box on the computer to make it not taxable to you. YOU need to check and be aware of your own taxes.

There are reasons, legitimate reasons, to take out some or all, of your 401(k). You can even 'borrow' against it. Again though, this is very rarely a good financial move. In the current economy, however, many people have had to take their 401(k) to live on. If, down the road, you find you need to do that, be aware of the tax consequences and be ready for it. To my knowledge, there is no way to avoid the 10% income tax they hold out when you get your check. Depending on your tax bracket, keep in mind that 10% may not be enough. If you are in a 15% tax bracket, you will owe the IRS 5% more to cover that withdrawal. Be sure you set that money aside so you don't get caught owing the IRS and you don't have the money.

For certain situations, you can avoid the 10% early withdrawal penalty. They will probably withhold the extra 10% when you get your check, but if one of the legitimate situations apply to you, be sure your tax return is coded properly by you or your tax preparer, and you might not have to pay the early withdrawal penalty on your return. Be sure you look into this before you take out your money so you are aware of what you will owe the IRS. A few legitimate reasons include withdrawing money for advanced education, certain medical bills, primary home purchase, and certain severe hardship expenses, like avoiding eviction or foreclosure. Just be sure you qualify *before* you take your money so you are prepared!

Here's to a Happy Retirement!

Self-trust is the first secret of success.
Ralph Waldo Emerson

Chapter 3 Worksheets

401K Plan

Kiplingers Personal Finance Magazine, April 2012, reports that if you start saving $200 a month starting at age 22, when you usually get your first full-time job, within 10 years you will have $37,000 (assuming an 8% return, a reasonable assumption for a long-term return on a diversified portfolio of stocks and bonds). 10 more years (age 42) you would have $122,000. Keep it up and by the time you retire at age 67 you would have a tidy $1.2 million. This is WHY you have to start young!

There are two 'usual' ways that an employer will 'match' your contributions to your 401k retirement plan. (Your employer may have one of these or they may have something completely different. Just be sure you understand how it works when you sign up for it. Ask questions!!)

Exercise 1
Part One

The first is a 50% match up to 6% of your gross income.

In other words, if you'll contribute 6% of your salary to your 401k plan, then your employer will 'match' 50% (½) of that.

So, if your salary is $50,000, how much is 6%? $_____
(50,000 x .06)

If your employer matches 50%, how much will they put into your account? $_____ (50% (½) of your 6%)

That is <u>free money</u> to you, so it's wise to at least contribute to your 401k up to the match.

If you are paid every 2 weeks, how much of that 6% will be coming out of each paycheck? $_____
(divide by 26)

You don't have to just contribute 6%. You can contribute up to your employer rules or the IRS laws. For 50 and under, $18,000, over 50 is catch up time and the max is raised to $24,000 (these figures are for 2015). If your salary is $100,000 and you contribute 15% to your 401k, how much annually are you saving per year? $_____
(100,000 x .15)

How much is your boss going to contribute? $_____

(Remember, 50% of 6%, not 50% of 15%).

How much needs to come out of your paycheck if you are paid monthly to contribute the 15%?
$_____ (divide by 12)

This may sound like a lot, but keep in mind, this is off-setting your federal income tax withholding. The more you are taking out, the less federal tax you are paying. IE: if you are in the 25% tax bracket, and you are withholding $150 a paycheck, your net out is really $115, since you are saving $35 in taxes.

Part Two

The second 'usual' way is that they will match dollar for dollar up to 5% of your annual salary.
So if your salary is $50,000, 5% of your salary is? $_____
(50,000 x .05)
How much is your boss putting in? $_____ ($ for $)
If you are paid every 2 weeks, how much will come out of each of your paychecks? $_____ (divide by 26)

If you salary is $100,000 and you want to save 17%, how much are you saving per year? $_____
(100,000 x .17)

How much is your boss putting into your retirement plan? $_____
(Remember – match is 5% $ for $ of $100,000 (not of the $17k)).

If you are paid monthly, how much is coming out of each paycheck? $_____ (divide by 12)

Exercise 2

Remember from the chapter, if you take out your 401k early, you will be paying a 20% total penalty. (10% for taxes, 10% for early withdrawal penalty).

You have been at your job for 5 years, and you have saved $80,000, and you withdraw your money. How much are you giving to the IRS? $_____.

Yup, you read that right. That's a FULL year of savings! Gone down the tube. Swooshhhhh.

If you roll over your money into another qualified retirement account, how much is going to go to the IRS? $____

And yes, the space here is tiny because the answer is 0.

So be wise, roll it over! Don't lose an entire year or more of you money!

<u>Back to Kiplingers</u>

The article referenced at the beginning of this chapter explains why it is so important to start early and save continuously. What if you don't start at 22? Kiplingers reports that in order to have that $1 million by the time you retire, assuming an 8% return, this is what you'll have to do:

Age 27
If you've saved $0, you need to save $263 per month.
Age 37
If you saved $0, you need to save $631 per month.
If you've saved $50,000, you need to save $254 per month.
Age 47
If you've saved $0, you need to save $1,636 per month.
If you've saved $100,000, you need to save $780 per month.
If you've saved $200,000, you need to save $125 per month.
Age 57
If you've saved $0, you need to save $5,376 per month.
If you've saved $200,000, you need to save $2,917 per month.
If you've saved $400,000 you need to save $459 per month.

Remember, no one cares more about your money than you do. Be smart, start when you are young so you can retire comfortably!

Chapter 4 - Budgets

Learning Objectives: At the completion of this chapter, the student is expected to:

1. Understand how to set personal financial goals.

2. Differentiate between needs and wants in evaluating spending decisions.

3. Investigate the student's money personality, including spending and saving propensity.

4. Develop financial goals for the short, medium, and long term that are specific, measurable, attainable, realistic, and time based.

5. Develop a budget that incorporates short-, medium-, and long-term financial goals;

6. Evaluate the impact of unplanned spending on a budget.

7. Develop a short-term saving strategy to achieve a goal such as establishing and maintaining an emergency fund;

Chapter Four

BUDGETS: SPEND SOME – SAVE SOME - GIVE SOME

Budgets. A word most people don't want to talk about. People I talk to say 'no way', 'not possible', 'don't need one', 'too hard', 'my spouse is just trying to control me!' and 'I wouldn't know where to start'.

    Budgets are not rocket science, but they do take discipline. And frankly, we are not a generation of disciplined people. We want it now, regardless of the consequences. The facts are that we *do* need a budget and it does take discipline because *it is* a matter of control. But YOU are doing the controlling, not your money controlling you. If it's just you, then you're in 'control' of what you do with your money. If you have a spouse/mate, then the two of you are controlling your money. If you have children, then there's control over their money too. Communication is the key. You and your spouse need to be on the same page when it comes to the spending, the saving, and the giving. (This is a good topic to discuss *before* you get married). If you have children that are old enough, you need to set the example and teach them as well. If they are getting an allowance, teach them to save some, save for what they want so they can pay cash –

spend some - (which teaches them to set goals), and give some. But children look to their parents for examples – so be a good one.

The thing is: budgets are a good control. When you *write it down*, you know what money you have coming in, and what is going out, and what you need / should be doing with it. You know what bills you have to pay, what you have for play, what you have to give or share, and what you should be saving. When you start spending more than you have, that's when debt kicks in and potentially gets *out* of control, especially when you don't know where your money is going. Recovery from debt can hurt – way more than the hurt that comes from a little self-discipline and a little control.

I'm not saying you can't buy things, or have fun, or even go in to debt. If you're going to have the 'American dream' of your own home, you will most likely have to go into debt. Very few people have enough cash to buy a house outright. Also, very few adults save enough to buy a car with cash. Both of these major purchases put you in with the majority of the American public. It is estimated that 80% of Americans are in debt, but much of that is housing or cars. Data released in 2012, shows 46.7% of Americans hold credit card debt, and the average *credit card* debt per household is $15,950. Ouch. 35 percent of Americans have debt in collections, which means they are not paying their bills on time. (Source: CNN Money, Controlling your Personal Debt, 2013). *Let's not become one of those statistics.* Make sure you can afford that monthly credit card, car or house payment *before* you buy it.

A budget is a way for you to succeed, for you to be financially successful and responsible. If you don't have a plan, if you don't write it down, it would be very difficult to become financially successful. Perhaps you're not convinced yet that a budget is a good thing. Here is a little bit of my story, and why a budget is necessary!

When my current husband and I first started dating, we had no extra money. We were both hanging on by a thread to pay our bills. I was doing a bit better than he, but he had more expense than I did. He had to pay child support, separate maintenance (similar to alimony), his rent, doctor bills, all the credit card bills they had, and still have money left over for food for himself and his children when they came for the weekends.

Dates were rented movies and popped popcorn at home. Or we'd go to the zoo, which was free at the time, or a walk in the park. We both had way too many bills to afford to go out.

Before we got married, we sat down with all his bills and made a list, the amounts due, when they were due, and the interest rate. We wrote it all down, added it up, and nearly had a heart attack. He had over $15,500 in debt. I had already made a list of mine by then, and most of my debt was in the form of mortgages for my rent houses. My first husband and I had built a rental house business and that was the majority of bills I had. I owed my attorney too, but I wasn't too deep in credit card debt.

The bad part about *my* debt is that in the rental business, if my tenants didn't pay, I didn't have money to pay my bills. There were many days that I would have mortgages due, and I had no money to pay them. Somehow, a tenant would show up and pay their rent, and I could pay my bills.

So ok, my bills were getting paid, and I could afford food – as long as I didn't get crazy and want to buy anything like steak or ice cream!

As soon as we got married, we took all his high interest bills – which was all of them, and moved them over to mine, which were relatively low compared to his rates. His credit had suffered during all of this and all of his cards were above 19.9% - ugh. One was 26.9%. Just moving those to a lower interest rate – I think all of mine were around 8.9 or 9.9%, helped. Payments could actually go toward the principal, not just the interest.

When we married, he moved in with me, so that eliminated his rent payment and cable payment. We knew instantly that we would take all of that money every month and use it to pay down his debt. But then we got serious about how to pay things off. We set up a budget. Since I was 'holding my own' in our house, with just a little money from his paycheck to help with more food, we decided we really could take the rest of his paycheck, every two weeks, and use every penny to pay off his debt. Now, being realistic, we knew he needed a little spending money in his pocket for things like a haircut, or if they were doing a burger lunch at work as a fund raiser, or something like that. We also decided that we would really like to be able to have a bit more entertainment – like maybe a matinee movie once a month, and if we worked it right, if we hit an early bird dinner special, we could probably eat out once in a while too! Oh, yes, we were excited!!

We started using envelopes. We had an envelope for groceries, at that time it was $150 for two weeks' worth of food for the three of us (my son included), his girls on his weekends, paper goods, soaps, etc. We ate a lot of casseroles, soups and stews. His 'play' money was $25 a paycheck ($50 a month) and our entertainment envelop had $25.00 for a <u>whole month</u>. We had a gasoline envelope, but I can't remember how much was in this one. I do remember that when we needed extra gas money for holidays with the folks, or family reunions, we'd have to scrimp and save from previous months to have enough to make the trip!

Clothes buying was minimal. I went to the thrift stores or garage sales for my son, who was then 6 years old. We have several thrift stores in towns where you can find clothes that are brand new with the labels still on them. My husband needed a new work coat, and yes, we found one for $5.00 at a thrift store in town. That was 19 years ago.

We lived like this for 18 months, just a year and a half. And in that time – we paid off all, yes, ALL of my husband's debt. The whole $15,500 + debt was gone. Additionally, my attorney bill of over $5,000 was paid off, my credit card bills were nearly gone, and the mortgages on the rent houses were all still on track, AND we had a tiny little bit of money in savings!! Was it hard?? Yes, of course it was. Was it worth it? Scrimping and just getting by to pay off the bills? Absolutely!

I remember the day we could make our entertainment envelope $50 a month, his spending money went to $75 a month, and the food envelope went to $175 every two weeks! It was a glorious day!! But we stuck to the envelope system.

You might ask, "If all the bills were paid off, why did you still need envelopes?" Well, now we had other goals. We wanted to start saving for emergencies, maybe take a short trip, not have to worry so much about the gas budget, and we knew he'd need another car sometime soon. We wanted to be able to give more, and we just needed a little cushion so we could pay our own way at family reunions, and a little money set for clothes – only on super sale of course! The envelopes hadn't hurt us up till then, so why not stick with it a while longer while we could build up a little cushion and sigh with relief? We used envelopes for several more years after that.

Create a Budget

Ok – so let's talk about creating a budget. If you look on the internet, there are tons of programs out there that can help you create a spreadsheet for your budget. Just upload all your information and they supposedly do all the work.

But, you don't need any fancy tools. A piece of paper and a pencil is all you need. The basic concept is to act like a business, money in is supposed to equal money out. I did find a nice budget worksheet at http:financialplan.about.com that you can print and use.

You have money coming in, and money going out, and the two should be equal, including your savings and giving. The younger you are, the easier this should be. Older adults just tend to have more bills. For example, a young adult may live in an apartment with all utilities included in their monthly bill. They would have a 'rent' payment, and hopefully 'renters insurance' which is usually a once a year payment. That's it for their housing expense. Many older adults would have a monthly mortgage payment, their house insurance, electric, gas, water, sewer, cable or satellite TV charges, and anything else I can't think of. Dealing with one payment is much easier than dealing with seven.

So, you're ready to start. To build a realistic budget, start by figuring out where your money goes *now*. Gather your bills and start writing them down. Start with a list of expected expenses like savings, charity, mortgage or rent, car payments, electric, gas, water, cable and/or internet service, trash pickup, student loan payments, credit card payments, day care and so on. End your list with the variable expenses, like groceries, gasoline, entertainment, clothing, eating out and gifts.

It's a good idea to track your spending for a couple of weeks or a month. Write down <u>every cent</u> you spend. Every cent. Soda at the store, pack of gum, lent a buck to someone, lunch – everything. Write it down. This is usually an eye opener by the way. When people see how much they spend on soda, coffee or lunch 5 days a week, they usually take a step back. HA! I did this in class one day. I asked the students who ate out and how many times a week. One male student and his girlfriend added it up to over $10,000 a year! That's as much as a good used car!

Once you know where your money is going, you can compare it to the money coming in. When projecting the amount of money you live on, don't include dollars that you can't be sure you'll receive, like year-end bonuses, tax refunds or investment gains. How are you doing so far? Do you have too much money left over, or not enough?

Now you need to set some goals. Are you saving? If you are, did you include it in your list of expenses? Financial experts say "pay yourself first." They suggest taking at least 10% of your income and paying yourself into savings for emergencies, trips, big ticket items, retirement, and things like that.

Another area to consider is charity. Do you have a favorite charity you give to? You need to be sure that's included in your budget.

Retirement? Are you contributing? If yes, are you contributing the amount you need/ want to?

You only have so much money, you want it to work for you since you worked so hard for it! Are you wasting too much on coffee or soda, clothes, entertainment? It's decision time!

<u>Columns</u>

You need 2 columns. A 'monthly actual amount' and a 'monthly budget amount'. The monthly actual is where your money is going now. The monthly budget column will eventually become your budget once you modify the actual column.

You modify the actual column so that you end up with a balanced budget. If you don't have savings, you need to modify – find money somewhere in the actual column that can be shifted to the second column. Even if you have enough money to cover everything listed in the 'actual' column, you may still need to modify. If you need retirement, you need to modify your income and participate in your company 401k plan, and/or contribute to a Roth IRA. Do you want to give to charity, and you can't? You need to find where you are spending too much money and – yes, you've got it – modify.

Experts recommend how our monthly income / paycheck should be spent on which expense. One list I found is (and there are many out there – but they are all essentially in this same area):

Housing and Debt (home insurance, mortgage and utilities) 30%, Taxes 25%, Insurance 4%, Savings and Investments 15%, and Living Expenses 26%. Add them together and you get 100%.

Many of the 'necessary' costs are non-variables. Your rent or house payment – you can't change (well, you can if you refinance, but I'll come back to that). Your car payment – you can't change (again, unless you refinance it). Expenses you can't change, stay in both columns. If you don't have a savings account, you need to put an amount in your budget column. Would you like a clothes budget? Then put one in.

That being said, be sure you DO budget for clothing, entertainment, going out to dinner, or whatever else it is you love to do! The key is to do it in moderation and to set limits.

The amazing thing is that by budgeting for fun stuff, it actually liberates you to spend money on these items. When you have money budgeted each month to buy clothes, the money is now sitting there waiting to be used for that assigned purpose. Suddenly you can go clothes shopping without feeling guilty!!

IF your spending exceeds your income, then you need to cut your spending. Look first for small savings - not because they'll end your budget problems, but simply because they're easy to find and take advantage of. Cut out that pastry or expensive latte. If you're spending too much on clothes or furnishings, shop only during sales. Do you need Netflix *and* HBO? Can you bathe your animals instead of paying someone else to do it? Can you start carrying a lunch instead of buying one every day and treat yourself on Fridays only. Have dessert at home after eating out. Better yet, stop eating out and cook at home! Higher gasoline prices make it a good idea to "bundle" shopping trips. Keep your house warmer in summer and cooler in winter. Take on chores that you usually pay someone else to do, such as mowing the lawn or shoveling snow. Use the public library for renting books and dvds, shop at thrift stores, and start using coupons at the grocery store! These savings will add up quick.

By the way, a great tip for managing your food budget is to make a menu for the week. List what you plan on eating every night, including your left overs, make a grocery list for what you need, and that's what you buy. It is really helpful because you don't buy stuff you don't need trying to guess what you need for the week. Post your list on your refrigerator. This helps with time budgeting too. Just look at your list and you know what you're eating and so does the rest of your family. If they want to know 'what's for dinner?' – tell them to check the list! This was crucial for us in the earlier days. If the kids wanted to eat left overs for lunch, they just had to check the list and see if we needed them for another dinner meal or if they were free game!

Remember, you don't have to give up everything just because you are trying to balance your budget and save money. You just need to get creative, like have a picnic in a park instead of going out to eat, don't forget the Frisbee! Check the internet for restaurant coupons or use early bird specials. Rent a free movie at the library and pop your own popcorn. If you get creative, you're not going to be missing out on anything.

Often it takes two or three revisions before you achieve a budget that you can really stick to. If juggling the numbers leaves you wishing you could free up some extra cash, then figure out what you can cut back on so you have that cash. When you SEE it written down, it is a lot easier to 'find' the money! But don't give yourself unreachable goals! If you need to make savings a 5% goal right now so you can work down your other debt then do it. When some of that other money is freed up, then you can up your savings.

Bigger Changes

If your money is way out of balance and adjusting your budget and cutting back isn't enough, you may have to consider changing some big expenses. Many people will consider this to be painful!

First, STOP using your debit and credit cards and develop your own envelope system, live on cash only. When your envelopes are empty, that's it till the next payday. No running to the bank with the debit card and withdrawing more money.

Depending on your interest rate on your house, you may be able to reduce your interest rate which in turn would lower your payment. Check with your mortgage lender. You may even need to sell that big house and get one you can afford. Perhaps you need to trade your luxury car for a smaller one that gets better gas mileage? Perhaps you just don't need to buy another car right now at all. Take care of your car so it last longer. Don't buy season tickets to anything for a while, and if you smoke, maybe you could take steps to stop smoking. Cut out anything that isn't necessary for survival.

You may have to take on another job for extra income. I didn't say it was going to be easy. If one is a stay at home mom, maybe she could do some babysitting? Get creative if you need to get more money into the house. How about a garage sale? Most of us have way to much clutter/ junk in our house or garage. Do you have a storage unit? How much are you paying for that? And what is in it you need? Maybe empty it out and sell everything.

Take your budget seriously. You need to check it every so often and tweak it as necessary. For instance, around the holidays you might need more money for groceries, but you could probably take that money from your entertainment column, because you'll be spending more time at home with family! As you pay off debt, you need to modify the budget and put that money in another column.

And by the way, if you have several credit cards, be sure you keep making your minimum payments on all of them. Take the one with the highest interest rate (not the highest balance) and put extra money on that one. When that card is paid off, take that money and add it to the payment for the next highest card. And just keep working it down till they are all paid off.

If you get a raise, that's another good time to modify the budget. If you still have a lot of debt, use the raise to keep paying your debt down. You've been living without the raise up till then, so you're not going to miss it if you put it on bills.

The lesson here: learn how to live within your means. Don't spend money you don't have. I see too many people that keep buying bigger and bigger cars or houses. Why? Who are they trying to impress? I tell my students to be careful what they wish for. If they want to "keep up with the Joneses" they'd better be sure the "Joneses" are paying their bills! If you don't think you have enough, stop for just a minute and look behind you – someone somewhere has less than you. Appreciate and be grateful for what you've got. If you do, you'll sleep a lot better!

Here's to a balanced life!

Without hard work nothing grows but weeds. ~ Gordon B. Hinckley

The most handicapped person in the world is a negative thinker.
~ Unknown

Chapter 4 Worksheets

Budgets

Exercise 1: Create a <u>balanced</u> monthly budget based on a full time, 40 hour week minimum wage ($7.25) job. Remember to take out approximately 15% for Federal income taxes, and Social Security, Medicare taxes. Fill in as many spots as you think necessary, add columns you need, or modify the ones listed here. (You may substitute your own budget if you have one).
(In this exercise, you only need to create a 'budget' column/)

Exercise 2: Create a balanced monthly budget based a full time, 40 hour week, wage ($18.00) job. Remember to take out approximately 20% for Federal income taxes, and Social Security, Medicare taxes.

Fill in as many spots as you think necessary, add columns you need. Make sure on this one you have emergency savings and savings for retirement.

Budget 1	Monthly Actual Amount	Monthly Budget Amount
INCOME: WAGES YOU EARN		
$XXXX.XX		
EXPENSES:		
HOUSE: Mortgage or Rent		
Homeowners/Renters Insurance		
UTILIITES: Electricity		
Water and Sewer		
Natural Gas or Oil		
Telephone (Land Line, Cell)		
FOOD: Groceries		
Eating Out, Lunches, Snacks		
HEALTH & MEDICAL		
Insurance (medical,dental,vision)		
Unreimbursed Medical Expenses, Copays		
TRANSPORTATION:		
Car Payments		
Gasoline/Oil		
Auto Repairs/Maintenance/Fees		
Auto Insurance		
Other Transportation (tolls, bus, subway, taxis)		
DEBT PAYMENTS:		
Credit Cards		
Student Loans		
ENTERTAINMENT/RECREATION:		
Vacations		
Pets		
Clothing		
INVESTMENTS AND SAVINGS:		
401(K)or IRA		
Savings		
Emergency Fund		
MISCELLANEOUS:		
Toiletries, Household Products		
Gifts/Donations		
Grooming (Hair, Make-up, Other)		
Miscellaneous Expense		

Total Expenses		
Total Income – Total Expenses		

Budget 2	Monthly Actual Amount	Monthly Budget Amount
INCOME: WAGES YOU EARN		
$XXXX.XX		
EXPENSES:		
HOUSE: Mortgage or Rent		
Homeowners/Renters Insurance		
UTILIITES: Electricity		
Water and Sewer		
Natural Gas or Oil		
Telephone (Land Line, Cell)		
FOOD: Groceries		
Eating Out, Lunches, Snacks		
HEALTH & MEDICAL		
Insurance (medical,dental,vision)		
Unreimbursed Medical Expenses, Copays		
TRANSPORTATION:		
Car Payments		
Gasoline/Oil		
Auto Repairs/Maintenance/Fees		
Auto Insurance		
Other Transportation (tolls, bus, subway, taxis)		
DEBT PAYMENTS:		
Credit Cards		
Student Loans		
ENTERTAINMENT/RECREATION:		
Vacations		
Pets		
Clothing		
INVESTMENTS AND SAVINGS:		
401(K)or IRA		
Savings		
Emergency Fund		
MISCELLANEOUS:		
Toiletries, Household Products		
Gifts/Donations		
Grooming (Hair, Make-up, Other)		
Miscellaneous Expense		

Total Expenses		
Total Income – Total Expenses		

Was this budget easier making ends meet? _____

What did you have to change? _____

Based on these two scenarios, how much money do you think you need to make an hour in order to live the lifestyle you'd like? _____

Exercise 3

Google "Reality Check" and your state. (ie: Reality check Texas)

Follow the instructions throughout and see how much money you will need to live on based on how you said you wanted to live. How much is that? _____

Exercise 4

Have a class discussion on what happens to your budget if you do NOT have an emergency fund. How quickly/ easily it is to go into debt with unexpected expenses occur.

Chapter 5 – Credit and Debit Cards

Learning Objectives: At the completion of this chapter, the student is expected to:

1. Compare and contrast sources of credit such as banks, merchants, peer-to-peer, payday loans, and title loans;
2. Compare and contrast types of credit, including revolving and installment credit, and collateralized loans versus unsecured credit; and
3. Evaluate the impact of credit decisions on monthly budget, income statement, and net worth statement.
4. Discuss how character, capacity, and collateral can adversely or positively impact an individual's credit rating and the ability to obtain credit;
5. Identify factors that could lead to bankruptcy such as medical expenses, job loss, divorce, or a failed business; and
6. Appraise the impact of borrowing decisions on credit score, including consequences of poor credit management and bankruptcy.
7. Differentiate between the use and cost of debit and credit cards.

Use mathematical processes to:

1. Analyze data to make decisions about banking, including options for online banking, checking accounts, overdraft protection, processing fees, and debit card/ATM fees
2. Use formulas to generate tables to display series of payments for loan amortizations resulting from financed purchases.
3. Analyze personal credit options in retail purchasing and compare relative advantages and disadvantages of each option;
4. Compare total costs of alternative methods of payment such as rent-to-own, store credit, installment agreements, cash, bank credit card, and debit card; and
5. Apply strategies for making informed decisions about purchasing consumer goods such as comparing prices per unit, looking for sales or promotions, and negotiating price.

Chapter Five

CREDIT/ DEBIT CARDS AND PAYMENTS

Credit cards. Wanted by all? Or hated by all? Hopefully you will fall somewhere in the middle. Once you start college, you will be deluged with credit card offers. I had to laugh when my husband in his late 40's was getting mail "to the parents of" offering credit cards for students! I asked him if he wanted to forward them to his parents!

Let's check the reality of credit cards. As reported by "The Survey of Consumer Payment Choice," Federal Reserve Bank of Boston, January 2010, 609.8 million credit cards are held by U.S. consumers. In my opinion, credit cards are necessary. I know a few of my students have totally disagreed with this, but some of them admit that they are not disciplined enough yet and will wait until they feel they can control their own spending. I know people that like to pay cash for everything in order to avoid debt. That's nice, but *you're not building any credit*. To get to middle age and still struggle with getting loans because you paid cash your whole life, well, it just makes life harder.

So, unfortunately, they are a part of life. I've never heard any financial professional say they were not necessary. We need credit cards to help build credit, which is a necessary part of growing up. And no, it's not the only way to build credit, but for most young people, without a co-signer, this is probably the easiest ways to get started. Keep in mind, the better your credit, the better your loan percentage rates will be for buying a car, a house, or getting other credit cards. Also, believe it or not, good credit helps with your car insurance. They have determined that good credit equals a responsible adult, hence a better driver.

There are three good ways to start building your credit. If your parents have <u>good</u> credit, they can actually put you on their card as a qualified signer. Of course, discuss and be in agreement with what you are allowed to do with that card.

If you have a savings account, ask your bank/credit union for an application for a 'secured' credit card. That means that they will attach your savings account for the 'credit limit' amount on your card. For example, if you have $600 in your savings account, ask them for a $500 limit on your credit card. Chances are you will be approved because they have *your* $500 'securing' your credit line. If you default on your card, meaning you don't make the payments, they will simply take it out of your account, so they really have nothing to lose. Of course, you can't withdraw that $500 either. As long as your card is 'secured', that money sits tight.

Another good way to get a first card, if you don't have savings, is to start with a store credit card. A store credit card is sometimes the easiest to get once you have a job and have already set up your savings account and maybe a checking account.

Your store credit card, however, will probably be at a very high, and to me, a very unacceptable interest rate, say 25.9% or higher. Ouch. Never the less, if you use it responsibly and properly, you will build your credit, and not go broke in the process.

Once you obtain your first credit card, buy something. Something small, that you need, and reasonably inexpensive, maybe around $10 - $20 and charge it. Then put the card away for the rest of the month. DO NOT use it again. (Building credit takes discipline. Don't go crazy buying stuff just because you can!) When the bill comes in, pay it right away, in full. Write that check, and get it in the mail back to them. Do not wait till it is due, because then you will be late. Big mistake and I will come back to this.

Now, with your first month bill paid, go and buy something you need again, inexpensive, and on sale of course. Then, like your first month, put the credit card away. DO NOT use it again. When the bill comes in, pay it in full right way. Do not wait, and do not assume the postal service will get it there in just a few days. You want the extra time, the leeway to be sure they get your money. If you mess up and run into a time crunch, take the bill to the store or the bank and pay it there. That way it will be posted and paid on time. If you do this a few times, you are building your credit. The store is going to report that you, John/Jane Doe, are a good risk, they are very happy with you. You take advantage of the credit card; you pay your bill in full and on time. They are *thrilled* with you!! And you are being very responsible by building your credit. When you go to and apply for another credit card, the new store will be checking your credit, and they will see that you are a responsible person, you pay your bills, and they like people like you! You will soon be able to build up to the credit card you want, hopefully with much better interest rates. And that is the goal of good credit.

In 2010, Congress passed a bunch of new laws regarding credit cards. The biggest change was that people under 21 years of age now had to have a parent/guardian/adult co-sign for them. Their thinking is that the adults would know better and wouldn't LET the 'kids' get out of control in their credit card debt. MY thinking is now YOU know better regardless if you have a co-signature or not!

<u>Late Payments</u>

Let me go back a little and talk about being late with your payment. If you are late, several things can / might happen. One, your credit record will take a hit. Not good. You are trying to build, not destroy, your credit. And everyone checking your credit rating will see that you are a slow payer, not desirable in the credit industry. Second, you will be hit with a late charge. Eugh.

Who in their right mind wants to pay – wants to use their hard earned money, on a late charge? Many are $25 or more. That is throwing your money away simply because you dallied. Third, your credit card interest rate can increase. Yes, that's right. You are already paying 21% or more, and it will increase. *Additionally*, other credit cards you have may raise their rate too. In other words, you were late on Credit card A's bill. Credit card B and C notice the late mark on your credit report, and you get an increase in interest rates on those cards also. But you say, "Hey, wait a minute, I wasn't late on those!" Correct, but too bad. And you may not even get notified that they have increased. You call and complain, and they say, "In the fine print…..that you signed in agreement." Ok, you get the picture. Welcome to the real world. So, the message here - DON'T BE LATE!!

The reverse here can also be true. IF you have been making all your payments on time, and you've set up a nice little history for yourself, CALL the credit card companies and say, "you know, I've been a good customer making all my payments on time, I'd like to reduce my interest rate please." You might have to ask for a manager, but many times they will lower your rate. Again, a very good thing!

Now, here's another twist to being late. I have heard horror stories where people have sent their payment in what they would consider to be plenty of time, and they still got hit with a late payment. You need to be aware of all the dates surrounding your bill. If you notice this happening to you, you need to take action. I heard of one woman who noticed this happening with a bank in her town. So she started taking her payment *to* the bank before the due date. To her surprise, she was still hit with a late charge. So the next month, she took the payment and demanded the clerk post her payment immediately. See, the clerks were taking the payment and saying thank you, and there they sat. Deliberate or not, but without receipts, the customer had no proof.

Life Lesson #1: Who cares the most about your money? You do.

So if you notice this happening, you think you are paying/sending your bill in plenty of time, and you are still getting hit with a late charge, take action. When the bill arrives, jot the date down on the outside of the envelope. Next, send the payment off immediately.

Usually there are several weeks between the receipt of the bill and payment due date. But don't wait. If you still get hit with a late charge, and they are not in town where you can personally take it too, then send it off through the post office and get a signature guaranty as to when it was received. It's not very expensive to do this with the post office. Someone will have to sign for the envelope. Then, if you get hit with a late charge, make some phone calls. Now you have proof that your payment WAS received on time, and you want those charges credited back to you. Speak with a manager if you do not get total satisfaction with the customer service representative. Do not be intimidated by whomever you are talking too. You need to be satisfied with the situation. And don't be embarrassed to ask another adult for help, like a parent if you can.

Minimum Payments

We need to talk about minimum payments on credit cards. Minimum payment schedules are set up for whom? You? Sure, of course you. Who else? "What do you mean who else? Who else is in this?" How about the credit card company? If *you* make only the minimum payment, *you* make them rich! And I'm not saying you shouldn't make minimum payments, on the contrary, you MUST make at *least* the minimum payment, on time of course. But let's look at an example. Let's take that $150 shirt you bought.

Say you put that $150 on the store credit card that charges you 22% interest. Your minimum payment is only $10 month. Wow! You can afford that! You *LOVE* that shirt AND the store credit card. Yehawww! Slow down cowboy, reality check.

If you make the minimum payment of $10 a month (at 2% payback rate of balance) it will take you 18 months to pay that shirt off. A year and a half. Will you still be wearing that shirt in a year and a half? Maybe not. And, you will be paying an extra $27 in interest. Well, $27 doesn't sound too bad.

Now, let's look at a brand new, wide screen TV. You go to the electronic store, they are having a special and you apply and receive a credit card, 22%. But, hey, the shirt went ok. Let's go for it!! You buy the best TV, high def, all the cables, a DVD player, and throw in a Wii. You work hard, you deserve it. Right? Your total bill is $3000. You are told your minimum payment is *only* $75 a month, and as your principal drops, so will your minimum payment. Heck, you can afford that! Check out and take home that puppy!!

Life Lesson #2: Here's the reality check. If you only make the minimum payment, that $3000 is going to take you 374 months to pay off. 31 years. Yes, 31 years. I'll say it again, 31 years. PLUS $7,476.99 in interest – on top of the $3000. That's right, that bill just turned in to a lifelong payment plan, and the TV and accessories now cost you over $10,000. Ugh. That's the price of a used car! (Again, at 2% balance payback).

Now, say that instead of making that $75 minimum payment each month you make a $100 payment each month. And extra $25 devoted to extra principal. It now only takes you 44 months of payments, 3 1/2 years, and your interest is only $1395. That's a little easier to swallow. Is the $100 too high? Well, since you can afford the $75 a month to start, stick with it; do not go down as the minimum payment goes down. Pay the $75 a month and you will have your bill paid off in 73 months, or 6.1 years, and pay $2,456.62 in interest.

Don't believe me? Google credit calculators. You will find a host of different sites that offer all different types of calculators. Plug your numbers in, along with minimum payment, and then add a little to the principal payment and see what happens. This is another instance where *you* are responsible for your money. Be wise about it and make good decisions and informed choices. If you have a tough month and can't come up with the extra $25, that's ok. But get back to it as fast as you can. You are saving hard earned money by making payments greater than the required minimum.

One more thought regarding credit card interest rates. Those highly advertised sales that shout "No interest till 2019 (fill in whatever date here)" are very inviting. And indeed, they are "no interest" until the stated date. But, (and there's always a but when it sounds too good) you MUST pay off that item *before* that date OR they add back in ALL the interest that accrued up to that point and tack it on the bill. So be sure you understand before you sign on the dotted line.

Buying On Sale

Let me talk a little about buying on sale. How many of you buy on sale? C'mon raise your hand! If you are not buying on sale, this section is for you, and if you are buying on sale, this section is for you.

I am known as the "queen of sales" to my family. While shopping with my mother –in –law (which I love to do by the way!!) one day, she started laughing. I asked her what was so funny and she said I was like a homing beacon, I automatically head for the sales racks, whether I could see them or not!!

Now, I understand that there are some items that you cannot wait for the sale to start. But for me, that is a rare bird. I cannot remember the last time I paid full price for something. Why? I work very hard for my money, why would I want to pay full price for anything? I am not a binge shopper, and I plan ahead. So let's look at it.

Say you go to the mall and find a shirt you love. Great! Price tag? $150.00. Wow. It must be a great shirt. You say "I MUST HAVE IT!" And you shell out $150 plus tax, for the shirt. How long, how many hours, did you have to work for that one shirt? Say you make minimum wage or just above. Since minimum wage is different in different cities, let's say $7.50 an hour and you work part time because you are in school too. So, how many hours? Let's assume the shirt cost $162.00 with tax. $162 divided by $7.50 = 21.6 hours. Whoa. Nearly 22 hours to buy that one shirt. For part time workers, that's a whole week of work. Now, do you still like that shirt that much?

Two weeks go by, and that shirt is now 1/2 price. That shirt now is on sale for $75.00, with tax, $81.00. Do you still love it? That means you only had to work nearly 11 hours to earn the money for that shirt. If you really want to get sick about it, you could calculate how much tax is coming out of your hourly wages to pay federal withholding and social security, and that means you needed to work even more hours to earn the money, but I won't go there!

Me, I'm super cheap. I won't pay full price and I typically won't even pay if it's half off. I like 75% off or more. I like it when the stores have the final sales, plus an extra 15% off coupon. And no, that does not mean its 90% off – as much as I would love that! Take this example. If there is an item that started at $100, 75% off makes it $25. The additional 15% comes off the $25, or an additional $3.75 discount. The sales that absolutely catch my eye are the ones that are 80% off, then for the final weekend, you get an additional 25% off. So, my $100 item is on sale for $20, then take another $5 off. My $100 item cost me $15.

That's how I shop. How can I do that? I plan. I usually have the majority of my Christmas shopping done by the end of January. If one of the family's needs sheets or blankets, it's a perfect time to watch for the sales and store them. Come summer time, someone wants new patio furniture and their birthday is in October? Watch for the sales and store them. Children clothes? Way too expensive. I typically watch how the child is growing, and buy at the end of the season for next years' season. Just buy the next size or two. Or, hit a thrift store. There are so many thrift stores or exchange stores that you can usually find what you need there. Every time I've gone in looking for something, I usually find something brand new with tags still on it! And watch their sales days. What a bargain! Do you like to give stuffed animals? Buy the valentine animals after Valentine's Day, and store them.

Here's a hint for storing. I made the fatal mistake my first year of not recording what I bought and for whom. What a mess I had. Now, I make a list of who I need to buy for – Christmas, birthdays, secretaries, friends, etc.etc. When I buy something to go into my storage cubby hole, I write down what I bought and how much I spent for that item. Then I either mark the price tag with who it's for, I use a sticky note, or I label the bag to tell me who it's for. Then, one quick peak and I know! Keeping track of how much you spent is necessary when you are buying for your children. You have to stay equal in what you spend; you'll figure this out as you go!

Cell Phones

One other quick area that I want you to be aware of that can affect your credit immensely, cell phones. Nearly everyone has one now-a-days, but how many of us paid attention to the fine print that said what would happen if you cancel your plan before the time is up? Yup, that's what I thought. Not very many hands went up on that one.

If you cancel your plan before your time is up, you are breaking the contract *you* signed with them. You usually get hit with a huge final bill that includes a couple of hundred dollars as a penalty for breaking your contract. Ouch. IF you don't pay this, it WILL go on your credit report and it will affect your credit score.

You need to pay attention to the details. Do your research before you commit to a plan. Talk to your friends, find out who they use and do they like them. Most offer some type of family/friends calling plan, and of course it would be helpful if you got the same plan as your family and friends do, you can usually call them for free. Also, pay attention to what you order. Do you text constantly? Then you need unlimited texting. Do you need a plan that includes tons of internet time? They have all kinds and combination plans out there. Get what you need and you won't be shocked with a huge bill at the end of the month that you can't pay.

If you are planning an overseas trip, that's another whole topic so do your research before you use your phone outside the continental United States.

Student Loans

Student loans are another area that can slam your credit. You signed a contract saying you'd repay that money, and yes, you must repay that money. If you don't, your credit will take a hit.

Here are 2 articles with more information. If you're interested, you can check them out! Cut and paste in address line.

http://www.kiplinger.com/magazine/archives/digging-out-of-student-debt.html?topic_id=14

http://www.kiplinger.com/features/archives/changes-coming-for-student-loans.html

More about Student Loans in that chapter.

Credit Card vs. Debit Card

Though many people think a debit card is pretty much the same as a credit card, there are definite differences. Credit cards are just that, credit. You are buying now with the promise to pay later.

Debit cards are linked to your bank account so when you swipe that card, the money automatically deducts from your bank account. They provide a convenient alternative to cash, especially if you do a lot of shopping. Many banks offer "overdraft protection" that allows you to exceed your balance. But you might end up paying interest and extra fees on the money you borrow from your overdraft account, so be sure you understand what the consequences are going to be.

In the event of a debit card theft, you may only find out *after* the money has been withdrawn from the account. Once you become aware that your debit card is lost or stolen, you need to notify the bank immediately. The Electronic Fund Transfer Act gives you the right to dispute an error on your bank statement and gives you some protections. For unauthorized card purchases, your liability is capped at $50 if you notify your bank within two days of realizing your debit card is missing. But between two days and 60 days, you could be responsible for paying up to $500 of unauthorized use. If you wait more than 60 days, you will be stuck paying all the charges, which could cause you to lose everything in your checking and overdraft accounts. And, if someone is taking your money out of your account, that means other checks that you have written are now going to be bouncing and you're going to be hit with overdraft and/or bounced check fees. Ouch. Obviously, you need to be careful when using your card to avoid debit card theft.

If your credit card is lost or stolen, you have a little more protection. The Fair Credit Billing Act basically means you have zero liability for fraudulent purchases, poor-quality or damaged merchandise, or for merchandise that was never delivered. Also, credit card users are not required to pay any amount that may be in dispute, meaning the cardholder retains use of the fund for the amount in question until the issue is resolved. At least this way, your bank account is not dwindling to 0.

There are recommended times to use your credit card over your debit card. If you need to put down a deposit – like renting a car, hotel room or a piece of equipment, use your credit card. Online purchases, big ticket items – credit card because of the protection already mentioned. Even in restaurants, credit cards are recommended because many restaurants will leave the amount open – expecting you to add a tip. Way too easy to steal that information or get more money from your account. My sister recently used her debit card at a gas station. Her bank put a hold on her card because someone there tried to run the number three times! BUT, they didn't call her. So the next gas station she tried to buy gas, it wouldn't work. She had to stand in a gas station on her cell phone, with the bank (thankfully it was open) and figure out what had gone wrong. So, lesson here – be sure and hit the 'clear' button on the machines screen.

Many credit card companies will call you within a day of a 'weird' charge. Just last week, I received and email notification on some charge coming out of some Pacific Ocean island. When I replied, no, I didn't authorize, they called me on the phone and put a hold on my card. When I checked with my husband, he had bought some vitamins – supposedly out of Canada, but on the charge slip it was the middle of the Ocean! I let the credit card representative know that yes, it was ok – and the hold was released. If this was done on a debit card, no one was checking and if it hadn't been double checked, that money was gone. Lesson here? Be sure and tell your spouse when you're charging something coming from another country!

Credit card theft doesn't always happen within a normal time frame either. We got a call about 8 months after we had been on vacation on the east coast. Our credit card number had been used in a state that we hadn't even visited!

Also, if you are going to be traveling out of the country or even out of state, you must let your credit card people know you are going on vacation and will be using the card there until X date. Then they will be expecting charges. If you plan on using your debit card to get cash from ATM's in that country, be sure and notify your bank/credit union also. And, check with them on charges – be sure you're not going to get hit with excessive withdrawal fees, transaction fees, money exchange fees, etc. etc.

Careful Spending!

That which does not kill you makes you stronger.
Neitzsche

Chapter 5 Worksheets

Credit and Debit Cards

Time to see how credit card payments really work.

Exercise 1

You can start with this one for minimum payment.
https://www.bankrate.com/calculators/credit-cards/credit-card-minimum-payment.aspx

On that same site, you can use the credit card payoff calculator. Under credit cards, go over to 'get advice' – you will find this

https://www.bankrate.com/calculators/credit-cards/credit-card-payoff-calculator.aspx

You can use that to play with the years! Plug these numbers:

Say you have a credit card with $2400 charged on it. Your interest rate is 21.9%, change the 4% to 2%,. Please keep in mind that MOST store credit cards now, and if you have 'bad' credit – your interest rate will be around 28 – 32%!!

What is the monthly payment to start? $_____

How long will it take you to pay off this $2400 if you only make minimum payments? _____
How much total interest are you going to waste? $_____. Click on Report.
Did you have a heart attack when you saw this amount?
Was it worth it? _____

Part 2

Go to the Payoff Calculator. Since you could afford the $48 initially, keep making that payment. Put your #'s back in, and under 'Payment per month' put $48. Hit calculate.
How long will it take you now to pay off the $2400? _____
How much interest are you going to spend now? $_____

What is the difference in time between *only* making minimum payment vs. continuing to make the $48 a month? _____

How much interest will you save? $_____

Part 3

Go back to Payoff Calculator, put your #s back in, go to "Desired months to pay off" – and play around with that. We already know it will take 11 years to pay off the $2400 at maintaining the $48 a month payment. That still sounds like a long time to me – especially since you are paying all that extra interest.

Let's cut the time in half. Plug in 72 months (6 years) and hit "calculate." What do you get for a monthly payment? $_____

How much more a month are you going to be paying from the $48? _____

How much interest are you going to save? $_____

Plug in 5 years.

What do you get for a monthly payment? $_____

How much more a month do you need to pay from the 6 years? $_____

Plug in 3 years, now what is your monthly payment? $_____

If you'll notice, the 3 year monthly payment is not quite double the $48 a month you started paying. But how much interest are you going to be paying now? Over 3 years, you'll be paying $896 in total interest.

Compare that to the original – only making minimum payments for 30+ years. How much total interest was that? $11,752.66??? OUCH.

And if you simply double the original minimum payment to $96 – you'll be saving even more. You're total interest would be $834.25. And the amount you will save compared to only making minimum every month is $10,917.66. That's the price of a good car!

Play around with this calculator. You can plug in your own balances and your own interest rates.

Keep in mind, when you want to get out of debt, start with the credit card with the highest interest rates and pay that one off first. Then take the money you were paying on that card and add that amount to what you were paying on the next highest interest card. Keep cycling down to the next then the next and before you know it, you will be out of debt.

Better yet, don't get too far in debt to begin with. If you charge something, you should plan on paying it off in full that month, maybe the next. Why spend your hard earned money on interest??

Chapter 6 – Paychecks and W2

Learning Objectives: At the completion of this chapter, the student is expected to:

1. Analyzes components of compensation from employment.
2. Identify benefits such as health insurance contributions, retirement benefits, sick leave, vacation pay, flexible spending account, health savings account, workers compensation, life insurance, and disability insurance.
3. Identify taxes that are deducted from paychecks, including Federal Insurance. contributions Act (FICA) and federal income taxes.
4. Calculate gross and net pay using information on a paycheck.

Chapter Six

PAYCHECKS AND W2's

When you have a job, you will get a paycheck from your employer. Your paystub will have how much you earned for that time period, plus list the taxes taken out, and then tell you how much your 'take home' or 'net' pay is, that is, what you earned minus the taxes.

<u>When do you get paid?</u>

When you get paid will be different for each workplace. Some will pay you every week, some every two weeks and some once a month. Whenever you get paid, you need to remember your budget and set money aside to pay your bills.

<u>How do you get paid?</u>

Most workplaces today use direct deposit. It saves time and money for them. You will give them your checking or savings account information and they will direct deposit into your account. Most employees choose their checking account because then they can pay their bills directly from that account. You can also withdraw money for spending or use your debit cards.

Your pay stub will either be handed to you or it will be online where you would log in for your information. You might start a file on your computer where you can copy them into, so you will have a record of what you earned.

Your paystub should have a 'year to date' column that tells you the totals you've made so far that year, and the total taxes that were taken out. However you get your paystub, you should always keep the latest one. If something were to happen to the company you are working for, you will always have the latest record to help you file your taxes.

You would probably be looking at either just a paystub, or a mock up of something that might look like this:

```
Company Name                                          #123

Pay to the order of        YOU                        $354.62

  $Three-hundred, fifty-four and 62/100 xxxxxxxxxxxxxxx
  THEIR BANK                        DIRECT DEPOSIT

         0000  000000000000         BOSS SIGN'S HERE

  Employee: You          Gross Earnings          $550.00
  Pay Period: May 5, 20xx  Deductions:
                         Fed. Income Tax           65.00
                         State Income Tax          10.00
                         Social Security           34.10
                         Medicare/Medicaid          5.50
                         Insurance                 22.00
                         401k                      58.78

                         Net Pay                 $354.62
```

Every workplace has their own way of how they do it. BUT, you should always have access to how much you made, the deductions, and the total you will 'bring home' – your 'net pay'.

Deductions

Oh yes, all those deductions! Most of them you just cannot get away from. From the paystub example above, the Federal Income Tax, State Income tax, Social Security and Medicare/Medicaid are all taxes that will come out of your paycheck and go to the government. These taxes pay for the Government, Military, Social Security that is currently being paid to those collecting Social Security, roads, bridges, disabilities, etc. etc. There is nothing we can do about those. These amounts are based on how much you make.

Don't get these taxes confused with sales tax or property tax. Sales tax is a tax that is added, by your own state, on products you buy. You pay them each time you buy something. That money goes to that state, some of the money stays there, and then they send some to each county/city, for their share of taxes received. In most states, groceries and prescriptions are usually exempt from sales tax.

Property tax is a tax an owner has to pay on their land or house. Some states charge a property tax on cars, trailer, motorcycles, and boats too. So be sure and understand what taxes you have to pay in your location or when you are moving. If you don't pay your property taxes, the county/city/state CAN and WILL take your property away, even if it is paid off from the bank.

Insurance: Hopefully your employer will offer health insurance that will help you pay for your health needs. Your employer may pay for all of it, or for part of it – where you pay for some of it, or they may not even offer health insurance.

The 401(k) in the list – this is your retirement contribution for this pay period. Good Job!! Saving for your future!!

Other things you might find on your paycheck

Your employer may list many more things on your paystub, including how many hours you worked, sick time, vacation time, etc., etc. Here is a list of the most common things that you might see on your paycheck:

- **REG** - regular hours worked
- **OT** - overtime hours worked
- **Holiday** - holiday hours worked
- **Vacation** - vacation time paid for
- **Sick** - sick leave/time paid for
- **FICA** - Social Security paid
- **Fed Tax** - Federal Income Tax
- **State Tax** - State Tax
- **City Tax** - City Tax
- **WKComp** - workman's comp contribution
- **Saving** - money you are putting in savings
- **Insurance/Medical** - insurance you are paying for
- **Life** - life insurance you are paying for
- **401(k)/retirment** - retirement contribution

- **Gross Pay** - the amount of money you make before deductions
- **Net Pay** - the amount of money you make after deductions
- **YTD** - Year To Date

The YTD column should have a total of what you have been paid <u>and</u> the total for all the deductions that have come out of your paycheck so far to date. This is the column we would use if something happened and you didn't get a W2 from a workplace at the end of the year. This is why you must hold on to your most recent paystub as you go along.

<u>Bottom Line</u>

You can see by all the deductions, that what you make at work is NOT going to be what you bring home and what you can spend. You need to remember this when you do your budget (see the budget Chapter 4). And remember, if you have questions – ASK someone!!

<u>W-2</u>

At the end of the year, you will get a W-2 form. Your employer is supposed to give you this form, mail it or have it online for you, by the last day of January in the New Year. For example, if you work during 2017, your employer has to either mail your W2 to you or let you have access to it online by the end of January 2018.

<u>What is a W-2?</u>

If you are an employee, you should receive a W2. A W-2 is an IRS form that you use to file your Income Taxes every year. When you fill out your 1040, 1040A or 1040 EZ IRS form, or when you have someone fill it out for you, you will need your W-2 from your job.

This form is VERY important! Put it in a SAFE place when you get it and DON'T lose it! Your W-2 has all the information for the whole year from your job. It has the total amounts you earned, the total taxes that were paid, how much you saved for retirement, and things like that. If you compare your last pay stub to this, they should match.

(www.irs.gov)

One for each job

You should get one W-2 for EACH job you had during the year. If you had more than one job, then you need to wait till you have all your W-2s from each job you had that year, before you have your taxes done.

If you don't get a W-2 from one of your workplaces, can use your last pay stub to get the information. This can be used to do a substitute W-2 if you don't get one. Just take your last pay stub with you when you have your taxes done. you

Some people think that if you are too young or too old, you don't have to file taxes. This is not true. Regardless of how old you are or how young you are or if you're a student, if you made over a certain amount of money, you need to file your return. Also, even if you didn't make over that amount of money, if they took Federal Income tax out on the money you earned, you should get that money back. So it will be good to check and see if you have to file and if you can get that money back.

Happy Filing!

It's not what you are that holds you back, it's what you think you are not. ~ Denis Waitley, author

Chapter 6 Worksheet

Paycheck and W2

Exercise 1

Instruct the students to research the jobs they want to have when they grow up. Then, discuss in the classroom. What type of education do they need? How much money do they expect in the first year? What is the minimum and maximum they can make in that position? Are there any laws regarding who can have that job? (Some jobs will not allow a felon to hold a license. This affects many jobs.)

Exercise 2

Discuss and practice job interviewing skills. Discuss appropriate dress for the interview. Students can practice handshakes, introducing themselves, and talk about previous experience. Proper dress would include button down shirts, long pants, sneakers (not flip flops), etc.

Chapter 7 – Personal Income Tax

Learning Objectives: At the completion of this chapter, the student is expected to:

Use mathematical processes to:

1. Understand filing of personal income tax.
2. Solve problems involving personal taxes.

Chapter Seven

INCOME TAX

It is said that there are only three things certain in life. You are born. You will die. And you will pay taxes.

As a student, in high school and college, there are many factors involved with how you file your tax return:

1. Whether you are still counted as a dependent (a qualifying child) of your parents – or not.

2. Where you live.

3. You're filing status: single or married.

4. How much money you earn – wages, interest, dividends, other.

A few terms you need to know before we go any further: Standard deduction, Personal exemption, Interest and Dividend Income.

Each and every 'person' gets a <u>Personal Exemption</u>. A personal exemption is an amount that a resident taxpayer is entitled to claim as a tax deduction against personal income when calculating taxable income. For 2017 taxes (which will be filed by April 15 of 2018), the amount will be $4050. When you are claimed as a dependent on another person's return, parents for example, you do NOT claim YOUR personal exemption, your parents do, even if you have to file your own tax return. The <u>Standard Deduction</u> is a little more complicated. Taxpayers make a choice to choose to claim the standard deduction OR itemize their deductions on a Schedule A. You would add up the dollar value of each tax deduction, and if it is more than the standard deduction, you would use your Schedule A. If the total is not more than the standard deduction, you would just use the given standard deduction. Charitable giving, mortgage interest, some medical bills are a few of the items on a Schedule A. For 2017 the standard deductions are $6350 for single and $12,700 married filing joint. You, if you are a dependent on your parents return, will NOT take the personal exemption, but you WILL take the Standard Deduction.

This is a good place to say that you do not need to file a Schedule A to take the 'Adjustments to Income': Traditional IRA contributions, student loan interest, tuition and fees, moving expenses, educator expenses and alimony paid. You will still take these deductions in the 'Adjustments to Income' on the bottom of page 1 of a 1040.

Only approximately 30% of the filing population chose to itemize using a Schedule A. If you do not have a mortgage with interest being paid, or have very large charitable contributions, you too will probably use the standard deduction and not itemize on a Schedule A.

The standard deduction for an individual who can be claimed as a dependent on another person's tax return is generally limited to the greater of:
- $1,050, or
- The individual's earned income for the year plus $350 (but not more than the regular standard deduction amount, generally $6,300).

The IRS allows the $350.00 deduction toward interest and dividends.

Example 1

Michael is 16 years old and single. His parents can claim an exemption for him on their 2016 tax return. He has interest income of $780 and wages of $150. He has no itemized deductions. Michael uses the second page of the 1040EZ to find his standard deduction. He enters $150 (his earned income) on Line 1 of his 1040EZ. Then $500 ($150 + $350) on line A (page 2 – Worksheet for line 5), $1,050 (the larger of $500 and $1,050) on line C, and $6,300 on line D. His standard deduction, on line E, is $1,050 (the smaller of $1,050 and $6,300).

Example 2

Joe, a 22-year-old full-time college student, can be claimed as a dependent on his parents' 2016 tax return. Joe is married and files a separate return. His wife doesn't itemize deductions on her separate return. Joe has $1,500 in interest income and wages of $3,800. He has no itemized deductions. Joe finds his standard deduction by using the second page of the 1040EZ. He enters his earned income, $3,800, on line 1 of the 1040EZ. He adds lines 1 to Line A and enters $4,150 on line A. On line C, he enters $4,150, the larger of lines A and B. Because Joe is married filing a separate return, he enters $6,300 on line D. On line F he enters $4,150 as his standard deduction because it is smaller than $6,300, the amount on line D. Joe will be paying income tax on the $1150difference between total interest income and the $350 allowed by the IRS.

The good news is that most people today will use some computer program to do their taxes. Just be sure you put you answer all the questions and the program will do all the calculations for you!

Interest Income

Interest income is revenue (income) received from a bank or credit union (or other institution) paid to you for leaving your money in their depository. You must pay tax on interest income from bonds, mutual funds, certificate of deposits (CDs) and demand deposit accounts (savings or checking accounts). If you earn more than $10 on your account, you will receive a 1099-INT and you MUST report it on your tax return. If YOU receive a 1099 – INT, the IRS is also receiving a copy of the 1099-INT and they will be matching numbers to be sure you are reporting the income to them. However, even if you do not receive a 1099-INT, you are still supposed to report the interest earned on these accounts. You will find that amount usually on your January statement, listed as interest income paid to you for the last year.

Dividend Income

Dividend income are distribution of earnings to shareholders that may be in the form of cash, stock, or property. Mutual fund *dividends* are paid out of *income*, usually on a quarterly basis, from *interest* generated by a fund's investments. Many Credit Unions report their 'interest' income in the form of dividends. You report these dividends with your interest income. If you have dividend income other than credit union interest/dividends, then you cannot file a 1040ez. You will receive a 1099-DIV for any dividends over $10 for the year. But again, any amount you earn – even if less than $10, you are supposed to report.

Qualifying child – are you a dependent?

The IRS states that:

A child (you) must meet all 6 of these requirements in order to be considered a Qualifying Child and be counted as a dependent for your parents.

1. **Relationship:** The person (you) must be a daughter, son, stepdaughter, stepson, foster child, sister, brother, half-sister, half-brother, stepsister, stepbrother, or a descendant of any of these, such as a niece or nephew.
2. **Age:** They (you) must be one of the following:

1. Under the age of 19 on the last day of the year *and* younger than you (and your spouse if filing jointly)
2. A full-time student under the age of 24 on the last day of the year *and* younger than you (and your spouse if filing jointly)
3. Permanently disabled at any time during the year, regardless of their age

3. **Support:** You must have not provided more than half of his or her own support for the year (regardless of who did provide the support). Support includes food, actual or fair rental value of housing, clothing, transportation, medical expenses, and recreation.
4. **Residency:** You must have lived with your parents for more than half of the year, except for temporary absences.
5. **Joint Return:** You must not file a joint tax return for the year (if he or she is married).
6. **Qualifying Child of More Than One Person:** If you could be a qualifying child for more than one person, the person claiming you must be the person who is entitled to claim you.

Bottom line: If you are under age 24 or permanently disabled, living at home or away for school, and only work a part time job, chances are your parents qualify to take you as their dependent child. If you only worked a part time job, your parents probably helped you with expenses. Even if you are married, you can still be considered a dependent on your parents return and you spouse would file a married filing separate return.

Obviously, there are many students that by age 18 they are on their own or emancipated. They would NOT be a dependent on their parents return, and they would file a return as 'single' taking both the dependent exemption and the standard deduction.

Or, if you earn a significant amount of money from a full time job, even if living at home, you probably will NOT be a dependent on your parents return. Your parents must prove that they provided more than half of your support for the year in order to claim you as a dependent.

I know this all looks very complicated. If you use a tax program to figure your taxes, all you have to do is check the box that you are a dependent for someone else and the computer will do all the work. Also, if you earned less than $6300, the standard deduction for single, you *technically* do not have to file a tax return. HOWEVER, IF they withheld Federal Income Tax, you SHOULD file a return in order to get all the income tax money withheld back!

The Social Security and Medicare tax that they withhold, you will not get back.

Most students are able to use the 1040EZ form if:

- Your taxable income is below $100,000;

- Your filing status is single or married filing jointly;
- You are not claiming any dependents; and
- Your interest income is $1,500 or less.

Chapter 7 Worksheet

Income Tax

You are a 17 year old student. You live at home with your parents who provide for the majority of your needs. Your income from a part time job is $1950. You received a 1099-DIV from your credit union for $18 for dividends earned on your savings account for the year. The W-2 you receive from your boss reports Federal Income Tax withheld is $187, Social Security withheld is $126.57, and Medicare Tax withheld is $39. You have no other income or deductions.

Based on this information, answer the following questions:

1. Are you required by law to file an income tax return? Yes or No? _____
   Why or why not? _____

2. If you are not required to file a return, why would you want to?
   _____

3. If you file a return, will you be claiming your Personal Exemption or your parents? _____
   Why? _____

4. How much money would you expect to get back? _____

5. How do you report the $18 dividend from you credit union?
   _____

6. Do you get your Social Security and Medicare tax withheld back? _____

Department of the Treasury—Internal Revenue Service

Form 1040EZ — **Income Tax Return for Single and Joint Filers With No Dependents** (99) **2016**

OMB No. 1545-0074

Your first name and initial	Last name
If a joint return, spouse's first name and initial	Last name
Home address (number and street). If you have a P.O. box, see instructions.	Apt. no.
City, town or post office, state, and ZIP code. If you have a foreign address, also complete spaces below (see instructions).	
Foreign country name	Foreign province/state/county	Foreign postal code

Your social security number

Spouse's social security number

▲ Make sure the SSN(s) above are correct.

Presidential Election Campaign
Check here if you, or your spouse if filing jointly, want $3 to go to this fund. Checking a box below will not change your tax or refund. ☐ You ☐ Spouse

Income

Attach Form(s) W-2 here.

Enclose, but do not attach, any payment.

1. Wages, salaries, and tips. This should be shown in box 1 of your Form(s) W-2. Attach your Form(s) W-2. .... **1**
2. Taxable interest. If the total is over $1,500, you cannot use Form 1040EZ. **2**
3. Unemployment compensation and Alaska Permanent Fund dividends (see instructions). **3**
4. Add lines 1, 2, and 3. This is your **adjusted gross income**. **4**
5. If someone can claim you (or your spouse if a joint return) as a dependent, check the applicable box(es) below and enter the amount from the worksheet on back.
   ☐ You   ☐ Spouse
   If no one can claim you (or your spouse if a joint return), enter $10,350 if **single**; $20,700 if **married filing jointly**. See back for explanation. **5**
6. Subtract line 5 from line 4. If line 5 is larger than line 4, enter -0-.
   This is your **taxable income**. ▶ **6**

Payments, Credits, and Tax

7. Federal income tax withheld from Form(s) W-2 and 1099. .... **7**
8a. **Earned income credit (EIC)** (see instructions) **8a**
 b. Nontaxable combat pay election. **8b**
9. Add lines 7 and 8a. These are your **total payments and credits**. ▶ **9**
10. Tax. Use the amount on **line 6 above** to find your tax in the tax table in the instructions. Then, enter the tax from the table on this line. **10**
11. Health care: individual responsibility (see instructions) Full-year coverage ☐ **11**
12. Add lines 10 and 11. This is your **total tax**. **12**

Refund

Have it directly deposited! See instructions and fill in 13b, 13c, and 13d, or Form 8888.

13a. If line 9 is larger than line 12, subtract line 12 from line 9. This is your **refund**.
If Form 8888 is attached, check here ▶ ☐ **13a**
▶ b. Routing number ☐☐☐☐☐☐☐☐☐ ▶ c. Type: ☐ Checking ☐ Savings
▶ d. Account number ☐☐☐☐☐☐☐☐☐☐☐☐☐☐☐☐☐

Amount You Owe

14. If line 12 is larger than line 9, subtract line 9 from line 12. This is
the **amount you owe**. For details on how to pay, see instructions. ▶ **14**

Third Party Designee

Do you want to allow another person to discuss this return with the IRS (see instructions)? ☐ **Yes.** Complete below. ☐ **No**

Designee's name ▶   Phone no. ▶   Personal identification number (PIN) ▶ ☐☐☐☐☐

Sign Here

Joint return? See instructions.

Keep a copy for your records.

Under penalties of perjury, I declare that I have examined this return and, to the best of my knowledge and belief, it is true, correct, and accurately lists all amounts and sources of income I received during the tax year. Declaration of preparer (other than the taxpayer) is based on all information of which the preparer has any knowledge.

Your signature	Date	Your occupation	Daytime phone number
Spouse's signature. If a joint return, **both** must sign.	Date	Spouse's occupation	If the IRS sent you an Identity Protection PIN, enter it here (see inst.)

Paid Preparer Use Only

Print/Type preparer's name	Preparer's signature	Date	Check ☐ if self-employed	PTIN
Firm's name ▶			Firm's EIN ▶	
Firm's address ▶			Phone no.	

For Disclosure, Privacy Act, and Paperwork Reduction Act Notice, see instructions.   Cat. No. 11329W   Form **1040EZ** (2016)

Use this form if
- Your filing status is single or married filing jointly. If you are not sure about your filing status, see instructions.
- You (and your spouse if married filing jointly) were under age 65 and not blind at the end of 2016. If you were born on January 1, 1952, you are considered to be age 65 at the end of 2016.
- You do not claim any dependents. For information on dependents, see Pub. 501.
- Your taxable income (line 6) is less than $100,000.
- You do not claim any adjustments to income. For information on adjustments to income, use the Tax Topics listed under *Adjustments to Income* at *www.irs.gov/taxtopics* (see instructions).
- The only tax credit you can claim is the earned income credit (EIC). The credit may give you a refund even if you do not owe any tax. You do not need a qualifying child to claim the EIC. For information on credits, use the Tax Topics listed under *Tax Credits* at *www.irs.gov/taxtopics* (see instructions). If you received a Form 1098-T or paid higher education expenses, you may be eligible for a tax credit or deduction that you must claim on Form 1040A or Form 1040. For more information on tax benefits for education, see Pub. 970.

  Caution: If you can claim the premium tax credit or you received any advance payment of the premium tax credit in 2016, you must use Form 1040A or Form 1040.
- You had only wages, salaries, tips, taxable scholarship or fellowship grants, unemployment compensation, or Alaska Permanent Fund dividends, and your taxable interest was not over $1,500. But if you earned tips, including allocated tips, that are not included in box 5 and box 7 of your Form W-2, you may not be able to use Form 1040EZ (see instructions). If you are planning to use Form 1040EZ for a child who received Alaska Permanent Fund dividends, see instructions.

Filling in your return

If you received a scholarship or fellowship grant or tax-exempt interest income, such as on municipal bonds, see the instructions before filling in the form. Also, see the instructions if you received a Form 1099-INT showing federal income tax withheld or if federal income tax was withheld from your unemployment compensation or Alaska Permanent Fund dividends.

For tips on how to avoid common mistakes, see instructions.

Remember, you must report all wages, salaries, and tips even if you do not get a Form W-2 from your employer. You must also report all your taxable interest, including interest from banks, savings and loans, credit unions, etc., even if you do not get a Form 1099-INT.

Worksheet for Line 5 — Dependents Who Checked One or Both Boxes

Use this worksheet to figure the amount to enter on line 5 if someone can claim you (or your spouse if married filing jointly) as a dependent, even if that person chooses not to do so. To find out if someone can claim you as a dependent, see Pub. 501.

A. Amount, if any, from line 1 on front . . . .
  + _____ 350.00 Enter total ▶ A. _____
B. Minimum standard deduction . . . . B. __1,050__
C. Enter the **larger** of line A or line B here . . . . C. _____
D. Maximum standard deduction. If **single**, enter $6,300; if **married filing jointly**, enter $12,600 . D. _____
E. Enter the **smaller** of line C or line D here. This is your standard deduction . . . . E. _____
F. Exemption amount.
  • If single, enter -0-.
  • If married filing jointly and —
    —both you and your spouse can be claimed as dependents, enter -0-.
    —only one of you can be claimed as a dependent, enter $4,050.   } F. _____
G. Add lines E and F. Enter the total here and on line 5 on the front . . . . G. _____

(keep a copy for your records)

If you did not check any boxes on line 5, enter on line 5 the amount shown below that applies to you.
- Single, enter $10,350. This is the total of your standard deduction ($6,300) and your exemption ($4,050).
- Married filing jointly, enter $20,700. This is the total of your standard deduction ($12,600), your exemption ($4,050), and your spouse's exemption ($4,050).

Mailing Return

Mail your return by **April 18, 2017**. Mail it to the address shown on the last page of the instructions.

www.irs.gov/form1040ez   Form **1040EZ** (2016)

Chapter 8 – College and Financial Aid

Learning Objectives: At the completion of this chapter, the student is expected to:

1. Recognizes the costs and benefits of various types of college, postsecondary education, and training.
2. Analyze the relationship between education and training and earnings;
3. Identify types of costs associated with college, postsecondary education, and training;
4. Compare costs among postsecondary education and training institutions such as public universities, private universities, certification programs, and community colleges; and
5. Analyze the quality of education investment using measures such as academic reputation, selectivity and rigor in a chosen area of study, average starting salary of students graduating in chosen field, and likelihood of student graduation.

Use mathematical processes to:

1. Understand how, why, and when to complete grant and scholarship applications and the Free Application for Federal Student Aid (FAFSA) provided by the U.S. Department of Education.
2. Research various sources of funds for postsecondary education and training, including student loans, grants and scholarships, and other sources such as work-study and military programs.
3. Analyze the advantages and disadvantages of various sources of funds for postsecondary education and training, including student loans, grants and scholarships, and other sources such as work-study and military programs.

Chapter Eight

COLLEGE AND FINANCIAL AID

The notion of going to college may be a 'given' for some people. Like me. I grew up being told I would go to college and I did. Straight out of high school for four years. For you? Maybe it's not a given. Maybe no one else in your family has ever gone to college. You might be considered a 'first gen' – first generation in your family to attend college. This may scare you. Can you do it? Do you have what it takes? Can you afford it? Will your family laugh at you? Will you actually have to take grief from someone in your family because you want more in your life? I did. When I went back for my first Master's Degree, I had a family member say "Are you going to go to school for your entire life? (It had been 21 years since I had received my Bachelor's degree). Then she asked – "Aren't our lives good enough for you?" And I said "no." I went back to school, worked for and received two Master Degrees. And I'm not done learning!

So if your dreams require college, I'm here to tell you GO FOR IT!!

It may not be as simple as running down to your local college and signing up. Maybe what you want to do doesn't require a College degree, maybe you only need a certificate from a Community College. Perhaps you should be in a Trade School? Many Community Colleges offer the same programs as a trade school. You have to do your research.

Maybe you want to be a Doctor, Engineer or Lawyer and have the Ivy League schools in your sites. Be sure you chose the right school for your degree. Ivy League doesn't automatically mean the best choice for you. You must do the research to see which schools, public and private, that have the best programs for what you want to do. Also keep in mind that in many of those big schools, you are being taught by a Teacher's Assistant, not the Professor that you expected.

Maybe you have no clue what you want to do or be when you grow up! Is your family pressuring you to start college? Go ahead and start. Declare a General Degree (or whatever your advisor recommends) and start with the basic classes everyone has to take. Maybe something will click along the way and you'll be on your right path. If you really don't want to start college, talk to your parents about taking a year off. Work a full time job, pay them rent, save some money, and maybe by the time the year is up, you'll have a goal in mind.

Please keep in mind, declaring a specialty degree, taking classes that are only good for that degree, then changing your mind to another, taking some specialty classes for that degree, then changing again, over and over, will devastate your financial aid. You can only take so much time to complete a degree on financial aid, and you can only take x amount of classes. ALL of these specialty classes you jump in and out of COUNT towards those x classes. It may be years before you figure out what you want to 'be' – and by then you have already destroyed your financial aid and you will not be able to get your degree unless you pay for it yourself. If you want to start school, and don't know what you want to be yet, take the general education classes nearly all degrees need. Then you are not blowing your financial aid.

Cost – Classes, Books, Fees, Living expense, etc.

Price for college classes is a main consideration for you. Private schools are much more expensive than public schools. A university, or a 4 year institution, is much more expensive than a 2 year community college. And, of course, in state tuition is much LESS expensive than out of state tuition.

For example: According to www.collegeforalltexans.com (retrieved 8/2/2017), they list the college costs for 2017-2018 for public universities.

Texas A & M Commerce, resident of Texas, tuition, fees, books and supplies is listed at $9843. Out of state or 'non- resident' tuition, fees, books and supplies is listed at $22,284. If you need to live on campus, room and board, transportation and other fees add on an additional approximately $13,000. If you are in an apartment, it will be more than that. This was not the most expensive, nor the cheapest school listed for Texas.

For community colleges, in district, out of district, and non-resident are a factor in cost. Again, www.collegeforalltexans.com (retrieved 8/2/2017), Amarillo College with their tuition, fees, books and supplies is listed at $4342. This is in district. Out of state, or non-resident tuition, fees, books and supplies is listed at $7552. Austin Community College is listed as having a more than $10,000 difference in their in district versus out of state tuition and fees!

If you are comparing Texas A & M Commerce vs. Amarillo College for tuition, fees, books and supplies, there is a $5500 difference in just those expenses PER YEAR.

By the way, the average moderately priced private college for tuition only has been listed at $32,410. https://bigfuture.collegeboard.org/pay-for-college/college-costs/college-costs-faqs. This does not include the fees, books, supplies or living expenses.

Ivy League Schools tuition run from $49,000 to around $57,000. Add in fees, room and board and you are mid $60,000. https://www.ivycoach.com/the-ivy-coach-blog/tag/ivy-league-tuition/ .

Living Expenses

You may want to head off to college, escape the parents, run with the wind, experience freedom…but can you afford it? Perhaps you could live at home for the first two years of college and attend your local community college? Or maybe you're planning on taking all the financial aid and loans you can get your hands on in order to attend a university out of town.

Even that decision is complicated. Maybe you've been offered a 4 year scholarship for sports or your GPA. Obviously, you'd consider heading straight to a 4 year school. Perhaps the university is offering an incentive to start there and skip the community college. You need to consider that.

If you start at a community college and then transfer to a 4 year university, then be sure you work closely with your advisor. Let them know upfront that you are planning to transfer to be sure all classes you take at the community college will transfer and COUNT toward your degree plan at the university.

If you move away to attend an out of district college, community or university, you will be incurring additional living expenses. If you live in the dorm, you can expect an additional $7,000 to $14,000 for room and board. If you live on your own, you need to consider the cost of the apartment, utilities, cable, internet, food, furniture, pots and pans, dishes, etc. If you have a roommate, will you get along? Will they pay like they are supposed to? Do you/they like to party? Or both focus on your studies. Will you have a part time job? And the considerations go on and on. Even in a dorm room you have meal times to adhere too; floor mates that like to party while you are trying to study and other issues that will come up.

Either way, if you can stay at home and go to a local college, university or trade school, you will be saving 10s of thousands of dollars in just the first 2 years. In my humble opinion, if you can, stay at home as long as you can. You'll thank me later when it's time to pay the student loans back!

Trade Schools

A Trade School is also known as a technical school or a vocational school. Most trade schools offer degrees or certificates for skilled labor positions like machinist, mechanic, dental hygiene, electrician, HVAC, welding, pharmacy tech, etc. They do not require classes such as English, Behavioral studies, Government, History and the like. You will focus only on the classes you need to perform your job. The average cost of a trade school reported in 2016, is $33,000. You will be done in 2 years or less and start your career. This may be a perfect fit for you! Keep in mind that you may still require specialty tools (welding for example) that could cost up to an additional $10,000 or more.

Many think a trade school is a good option. You get out faster, you start your career, and the difference in money that you would make in salary versus a 4 year degree, which would take you 2 more years to complete, is considered to be made up due to the earlier start of your career.

Now, compare that to a community college. Many community colleges offer the same vocational, trade degrees. You can get a certificate, if you can go full time, in about 18 months. If you want an Associate's Degree, you probably will take 5 additional classes (English, behavioral studies, 1 math, speech, and a language or philosophy) plus one elective, to finish off. You are still done in 2 years, and how much did that community college cost? About $10,000 for the 2 years? Plus you are still needing to supply your tools and equipment.

So if you chose a trade school, you must way the options between a trade school and the local community college. This is your life and your career. Take the time to do the research.

Move and Desire

Two more big decision you will need to make before you chose a career is – Will you move for a job? If you want a degree in nursing for example, are there plenty of jobs available in your local? Dental Hygiene? Welding? Are you going to have to move to get a good job, and can / will you? Do you have family that requires you to stay local? Children? Specialty services for your child? Elderly parents? Other family obligations? You can research the need in your area. Google and use social networking to see if there are jobs available in your area or where you'd like to live!

And oddly – another decision…do you want to be rich? Many people have grandiose visions of when they are done with college. Do you want to be able to afford lavish vacations every year or a staycations or a day trip out to the lake enough? Do you want to travel the world annually? Have you thought about retirement and what that looks like (and no, it's not too early to be talking about retirement)? Do you need a new car every year? Or will you drive what you have until it's paid off, then years and years to go without needing a new car? You need to decide what you want your life style to look like. Will you forfeit new cars every few years to take those great trips?

If you want to be lavish, be sure your career choice matches. Being a social worker – you're not going to be rich. You can be rich in retirement if you do it right, but until you get there, you will be on a budget. Teacher? Not going to be rich. Welding? Maybe. Will you go work on the oil rigs or help build high rise buildings? They make good money. Keep in mind also that even if you see a higher salary in, for example, Boston, the cost of living there will probably be way more than what you are paying now if you live in a small town or city. Just some thoughts to keep in mind!

Financial Aid

The *purpose of financial aid* is to provide funding for eligible students who want to attend college when their own personal and/or family *financial* resources are insufficient to cover that cost of attendance. Or, more simply put, the *purpose of financial aid* is to ensure that each student has sufficient resources to enable them to attend college. There are several forms of financial aid that you can receive if you are eligible.

The first step in getting any financial aid (except scholarships) is to create a FSA (Federal student aid) ID. Go to StudentAid.gov/fsaid to create your ID. Next, go to fafsa.gov (Free Application for Federal Student Aid) and fill out the application.

This application can be completed as early as October 1 of the year before you plan on starting college in the fall, or possibly summer classes. You would use the tax information on your parents return from the previous year. IE: You could apply Oct. 1, 2017, using the 2016 tax returns of your parents or your own if you are considered an independent.

School deadlines can differ. So be sure and go to fafsa.gov to research the schools you are interested in for their deadlines.

You must reapply for financial aid every year. When changing schools, your aid does not automatically transfer, so be sure and check with your new school to see what you need to do.

Once you submit your FAFSA, you will receive a SAR, Student Aid Report, usually within 3 days to 3 weeks. Be sure you double check your information to be sure you have not made a mistake. You may be asked to verify some information. The school that you are interested in can help you with that.

Sometime after the SAR, you will receive an 'award letter'. This letter will inform you how much aid you are eligible for from the schools you have listed on the FAFSA. This letter could come as early as the spring, or as late as right before the fall semester begins. It depends on the school and when you actually applied.

The amount of the award will be dependent on several factors: cost of attendance, amount your family is expected to contribute, year in school and enrollment status – full or part time.

You do NOT have to accept all the money offered. It is suggested you take the 'free' money first – scholarships and grants, then the work study money that you earn through a job, then the student loans – which have to be paid back.

The financial aid staff at your school will explain how and when you will get your money. If you are taking a loan, you will have to sign a master promissory note before you get this money.

Student loans MUST be repaid! You cannot get rid of these by declaring bankruptcy. This money is essentially coming from the Federal Government and they WILL get their money back!

Latest research (2017) reports that many college graduates cannot buy a house because they have too much debt that involves student loans. You cannot, or will not, qualify for a loan from the bank to get a mortgage if your debt to income ratio is too high. The average student loan debt in 2017 is over $35,000. That is just the average. Obviously a doctor or lawyer, or even a nurse practitioner, can have well over $100,000 - $250,000 in student loan debt. Except for a doctor or lawyer, one rule of thumb is that you should not be borrowing more than you expect to earn in your first year of full time work. If you are expecting to earn $75,000, you should not borrow more than $75,000. Keep in mind most loans are paid back in 10 years!

Student loans are there to help you go to college. Not for living on. Unless your class load is significantly over the suggested full time load so you can finish significantly ahead of schedule, or you are in an internship, a full or part time job should be expected to help with living expenses. Be careful with how much money you borrow!

Types of Federal Student Aid: Grants, Work-Study, and Loans

Federal Pell Grant: Does not get repaid; for undergraduates (in some cases a post baccalaureate teacher certificate); max time 12 semesters. See your financial aid office for more information.

Federal Supplemental Educational Opportunity Grant: Does not get repaid; for undergraduates with exceptional financial needs; funds depend on availability at the school. See your financial aid office for more information.

TEACH Grant: For teachers only with the agreement that the student will teach in a qualified need area. See your financial aid office for more information.

Iraq and Afghanistan service Grant: Does not get repaid; for students who do not qualify for Pell and whose parent or guardian died as a result of service in Iraq or Afghanistan after 9/11. See your financial aid office for more information.

Work Study: Money that is earned while attending school. Does not get repaid. For undergraduate or graduate students; jobs can be on or off campus.

Loans: Borrowed money for college or career school. These must be repaid with interest.

Direct Subsidized Loans: For undergraduate students. Interest is paid while student is in school by the Government. Rate, as of 2017, is 3.76%. See your financial aid office for more information.

Direct Loans Unsubsidized: For undergraduate, graduate or professional students. Financial need is not a requirement. Rates, as of 2017, run from 3.76% to 5.31%. See your financial aid office for more information.

Direct PLUS Loans: For parents of dependent undergraduate students and for graduate or professional students. You must be enrolled at least half time. Financial need is not a requirement. Rates, as of 2017, are 6.31%. See your financial aid office for more information.

Federal Perkins Loans: For undergraduate and graduate students with exceptional financial need. Interest rate, as of 2017, is 5%. See your financial aid office for more information.

For more information on interest rates, visit Studentaid.gov/interest. For more information in types of federal student aid, visit Studentaid.gov/types.

Earnings

Data shows education returns a much larger life time earning potential.

High school graduates, on average, earn $580,000 over their lifetime.

Associate Degree holders, on average, earn approximately $915,000 over their lifetime.

Bachelor Degree graduates, on average, earn approximately $1.19 - $2 million over their lifetime.

Master Degree graduates, on average, earn approximately $2.67 million over their lifetime.

Doctoral Degree graduates, on average, earn approximately $3.25 million and up, over their lifetime.

Chapter 8 Assignment
College and Financial Aid

Ask your local college or university to send a representative to come and speak to your class about the importance of filing a FAFSA form. (Many are already doing this and would be happy to come!)

Chapter 9 – Buying a Car

Learning Objectives: At the completion of this chapter, the student is expected to:

1. Analyze costs and benefits of owning versus leasing a vehicle.
2. Apply strategies for making informed decisions about purchasing consumer goods such as comparing prices per unit, looking for sales or promotions, and negotiating price.
3. Develop an intermediate-term saving and investing strategy to achieve a goal such as accumulating a down payment on a home or vehicle.
4. Explain the costs and benefits of automobile insurance and factors that impact the price of insurance, including the type of vehicle, age and sex of driver, driving record, deductible, and geographic location.
5. Use technology to create amortization models to investigate automobile financing and compare buying a vehicle to leasing a vehicle.

Chapter Nine

BUYING A CAR

Let's face it, for most people, buying a car is right up there with negotiating to having a tooth pulled! Car salesmen (and I'm including women here) are very good at what they do, that is *why* they are salesmen. Used or new, it does not matter.

My husband and I wasted an entire Saturday afternoon buying a car. It took 4 hours, yes, 4, FOUR hours to negotiate the price and sign the papers. I swore, from that day on, I would NEVER do that again, waste my time and play their games. And I have been true to my word.

Here's what happened. We were on the way to the movies, and decided, we had about 30 minutes to kill. We were kind of thinking about a new car, but didn't *really* need one right that day. That was our first big mistake. We saw a car and fell in love with it.

The salesman came out and said he would make us a great deal, and how much would we give him for the car? We hemmed and hawed and said $14,000. The price on the car was around $18,500. The salesman went into the building and came out 15 minutes later. For 15 minutes we are standing in the parking lot playing *their* game. He comes out and says "Ok, YOU WIN!! $17,850!!" $17,850? How is that an "I" win? This went on for 3 1/2 hours. Finally, the price we paid was $14,000, exactly what we said from the beginning.

Lesson 1. First; who are they (the salesmen) working for? You? Not. They are working for themselves. Do they care about your money? Sure they do. They *want* your money and they want as much as they can get.

How many of you have heard "How much a month do you want to spend?" Personally, I hate that line. Personally, I'm cheap. I don't *want* to spend anything. But I guess it is unrealistic to expect them to just *give* me a car. If you need transportation, and you have determined that a car is the best solution, then I guess you need a car and you will have to spend some money. So my goal is to give them as little of my money as possible. How do I do that?

Lesson 2: Do your homework. You have two homework assignments before you start to look. First assignment: research what car you want. You need to look around, watch cars on the streets, look in parking lots as you walk. Do you want something sporty? Economical? Convertible? Lots of storage? Bucket seats? A specific color? Automatic or manual transmission? How many people need to be able to fit in your car? Do you need GPS? A CD player (1 or 6?) Etc. etc. etc. YOU need to be prepared with what you want and what your needs are. And don't just think immediate future either. If you are about to get married and want to start a family right away, a two door convertible may not be the best option. Once you have a few cars in mind, get on the internet and see how the car holds up. Are the repairs excessive? Do they crumple in a collision or do they hold up in a wreck? What is the resale value? How about gas mileage? Do you travel a long way to school or work? Or just around town?

You don't have to be stuck in stone – but you should get something close to what you want and need, don't you think? Most of your decisions should be made before you hit the car lots.

Then, get back on the internet and see what the value of the car is, new and used. Check out the values with different options added or not added. You do the work, you figure it out. If you need to put notes on an index card and take them with you, do it. Don't trust them to save you money. This is your money. No one cares more about it than you do. Get a price in your head. A **total** price, not a monthly price.

Kiplingers Personal Finance magazine (January 2011) had an article that gave information on how to buy a car. Their suggestion was to use a service, like TrueCar.com (free service) to find the 'real' dealer costs. If you go to Kiplinger.com/links/dealercost you will find additional information on the 'real' cost of a car to a dealer, not the invoice price. TrueCar.com takes into consideration the incentives that have been offered to the dealers and you having that information can help you get the best deal on the car.

The second part of your homework, is to go to your bank or credit union and see what loan amount you qualify for. Tell them what you want or what you're thinking about, and see if they will loan you the money for a car. Find out what your interest rate will be and what your monthly payments, through them, would be. Can you get a discount if they do an automatic withdrawal from you checking or savings account? Can you afford it on a monthly basis? Check your budget.

Now you are informed and ready for the car lots. You know essentially what you want, how much it should cost and how much you will pay for it on a monthly basis.

Lesson 3: The best time to buy a car is when you do NOT need one *that* day. Try not to be in a position of being desperate. Shop when you have time and can think logically and rationally about it. If you find you are running out of time that day and still haven't found what you wanted, so what? Big deal. The exact car you want may not be on a lot that day. That's why it's best to not be in a bind when looking. Go again in a week. You're in control. YOU make the decision to control your spending and what you buy. Don't get intimidated. Especially the line (and I love this one!) "If you don't buy it now, it may be gone tomorrow!" I just finished car shopping with my sister and I cannot tell you how many times we heard that. Our response was "Well, if it is gone tomorrow, it was not the car for me."

Also, when *you* are not desperate, you can wait for *them* to be desperate. End of the month, rainy days, end of year before they have to pay the tax man for the inventory are all good times to buy. But if you are desperate, you cannot wait, you might buy something you regret later.

Lesson 4: You don't have to be rude, but if they don't have the car you want, move on. Your time is valuable. Don't settle for something you don't want. Salesmen are very persuasive.

My husband and I were looking for a specific van we wanted to buy. No dealer where we lived had one, so we decided to travel to a larger city. We went for one weekend. Three days. Three days is not a lot of time to scour a large city that might have what we wanted – especially when you add in the traffic of a large city. We checked newspaper ads and made phone calls, but mostly we hit every possible car lot we could find. Typically, there were two or three lots next to each other. My husband would go to one, I would go to another. Find a salesman and say "We are looking for da da da. Do you have one?" "No, but we have…" "Oops. Stop right there. That is not what we are looking for. Thank you for your time" and off I went to the next lot. My husband would stop and chat. I'd catch up with him, "do they have one?" "No, but hey have…" "Thank you very much, but that's not what we are looking for. Have a nice day." And I would pull my husband out of there and back to our car to hit the next set of lots. We knew what we wanted, so why waste our time (and theirs) looking at something we didn't want. Honestly, my husband hates to go car shopping with me. He says I'm too brutal. I have a price and I know what I want, and my time is valuable. How is that brutal?

Lesson 5- final lesson: Car dealers know exactly – yes *exactly* – what the bottom line is for that car. That salesman from the first story *knew* they could sell it for $14,000 when we started, but they wanted to get as much of my money as possible. They figured I would wear down, and accept their price.

Now, when we find a car we want, we give them a price and tell them they have 10 minutes. If they don't come out in 10 minutes, we get in our car to leave. Or, I should say, try to leave. They usually come running out and actually block our car. "Where are you going?" "I told you, you had 10 minutes." Ok, so perhaps this *is* a little brutal. But remember. They know exactly what they can sell that car for. They can either sell it for the price I'm willing to give or they are not. I am not going to play the back and forth game. And I tell them that. This is the price. Yes or no? It really is that simple.

So here's the part where you say "But what are they doing in there all that time? Surely they are trying to convince the manager to sell me the car for the price I gave him." Oh, you are so funny. They are going to the bathroom, making phone calls, getting coffee, donuts, whatever. But I assure you they are not negotiating the price for you. How do I know this? Well, I've had students that were car salesman, and I watched a well-known day time talk show that had car salesman on telling people what they are doing while *we* are standing in the parking lots.

If you are buying a used car, and you find one that you think you like, you should be allowed to take it off the lot and to your mechanic. Take the car to someone whom you trust to give it a quick look over. It doesn't take long, about a half-hour and they can visually look for leaks, cracks, wiggles, sounds and whatever else they look at. For my sister, this service was invaluable! She took at least three cars to our mechanic and they, with just a quick ride and quick visual check, could give her an estimate of what they knew was wrong with them. Of course there could have been more once they started working on them, but if the initial list is too long to begin with, you might think about passing on that car. One of the cars the mechanic said he wouldn't buy it and neither should she! So it does need to be someone you trust to be honest with you! If the car lot doesn't allow you to take the car to your mechanic, go to a different car lot!

Trust yourself. If you smell something funny, or the car shimmies when you get to 65mph, something's wrong. If it just doesn't feel 'right' – then pass. DON"T let the salesman tell you 'it's normal'!

One more hint if you'll permit me. BEWARE of the 'buy here, pay here' locations. My sister and I did stop at one because they had a couple of cars on the lot she was interested in. When we asked the price, they said "oh, around $11 or $12k." I cracked up laughing; I could not hold it in! We knew those cars should have been less than $6k (we had done the homework). When the salesman saw me laughing, he said "well, you buy it here and pay for it here." The interest rate was around 18% to buy that overpriced car. This is *not* a good deal. I have since heard that if you want to pay them off early you still have to pay ALL the interest you would have paid if you completed the contract to the end date. Again, NOT a good deal. You need to read the contract before you buy it. I'm not sure if they are all like that, but this is *huge* buyers beware! So just be careful!

Leasing a Car vs Buying a Car

Leasing

When you buy / purchase a car (new or used) you pay the entire negotiated price for the car, plus sales tax, title and license (TT&L) fees. Hopefully you have a down payment to reduce what you finance, and then, based on previous calculations from this chapter on what you can afford, you can finance the car for 3, 4, 5 or 6 years. (Hopefully no more than 3 or 4 years!!) When you lease a car, you're only financing the depreciation that occurs during the lease term (most commonly three years), plus fees. You pay sales tax at the end of the lease on the residual value (the expected value) of the car. Then, at the end of the lease term, you simply return the car to the dealership.

According to experts, this basically means that your monthly payment on a lease might be less than your monthly payments vs buying a car. However, keep in mind that you are renting this car, paying for something that you are going to turn back in in 3 years. You will have no equity in the leased car that could count towards your next car.

When you lease a car, there is usually a down payment that ranges between $1500 and $5000. Yes, there are $0 down plans, but these are rare. And with deposit or $0 down, you still have to pay tax on the deposit, and various acquisition fees to get the car. If you see a 0 down to lease a car, with no money in your pocket, you still will not be driving away with a leased car.

Mileage is also limited on a lease. They allow between 9,000 and 15,000 miles per year. If you go over this amount, you will pay a premium of up to $0.25 per mile you go over.

Repairs are usually covered under the warranty that comes with the car, but this comes with buying a car that has some warranty also. But, if you don't take care of the car, or are very rough on it, you will be charged additional fees at the end of your lease.

Leases only go to qualified buyers, which means those with good credit. If your credit is less than perfect, you may need to wait until your credit score improves, or you chose to buy a certified used car.

Edmunds.com has a calculator for figuring up what your lease will cost. But to have all the figures it requires for calculating, you've probably already been to the dealership and know the answer!

Buying

As stated, when you buy a car, you are paying the full price of the car over the life of the loan. You put down a down payment, maybe you have a trade in, and you need to pay the loan fees (bank fee), sales tax, title paperwork, and license. (TT&L)

By the way, you can make more money selling your car outright versus turning it in. In other words, car lots give you less for your car than if you would take the time to sell it yourself.

You are responsible for repairs, hopefully the car still has some warranty on it. But if you need tires or an oil change, it's up to you. Be sure you calculate this in when you are deciding how much you can afford for a car.

At the end of the loan, the car belongs to you. If you keep it up and take care of it, then your car could possibly last you a long time. (I've been driving a 2001 Toyota 4 runner for 16 years now).

One *drawback* to buying a brand new car, is that the instant you drive it off the lot, it depreciates as much as 11%, just driving it home. That means that a $20,000 car depreciates $2200 just going home!

Depending on the market it is usually better to buy a good used car versus a brand new one. During an economic downturn, however, if cars aren't selling well, they may lower the price of a brand new car just to move them off the lot. Do your homework!

BE CARFUL! I have already covered this in the chapter, but be sure you know exactly how much you can afford, taking repairs and insurance into account and DON'T go over it! Don't fall for the extended times to reduce your payments. Try and stick to the 3 or 4 year (maybe 3 ½ years?) to pay your car off. If you can't afford a car payment in that range, buy a cheaper car!! They are happy to extend your payments out 5 years so you can have a lower payments – but all that means is they are making more interest dollars off of you!!

When it comes to buying and leasing, there is no one-size-fits-all answer. You need to do your homework and consider all of the pros and cons. Look at your budget and be honest about your mileage needs, lifestyle, and credit history before you even go to a car lot!!

In my humble opinion, if you are going to be paying 3 years on a car lease, and you could pay off an affordable good used car in 3 or 4 years, I personally would just buy a car! But that indeed, is just my opinion.

Car Insurance

Car insurance requirements vary by state. So be sure you check for your state requirements.

Not all states require insurance, but they all do require that you meet a financial responsibility to be able to have a vehicle on the road, and that usually comes in the form of insurance. New Hampshire is the only state that does not specifically require insurance, but you are required to show proof of financial responsibility if you are in an accident. Some states require you to show proof of insurance when you register the car.

States also differ on minimum insurance requirements. Almost every state requires you to have bodily injury liability insurance to pay for the treatment of anyone you injure. Other states operating under no-fault laws will require that you carry personal injury protection to pay for your own injuries. You usually will be required to buy property damage liability insurance to repair the vehicles of anyone you hit.

Liability insurance pays for injuries to the other party and damages to the other vehicle resulting from an accident you caused. It also pays if the accident was caused by someone covered by your policy, including a driver operating your car with your permission.

This is the 'usual' insurance you must carry. In Texas, the minimum is 30/60/25. Which means $30,000 in bodily injury liability per person, and $60,000 per accident if more than one person was injured in the accident. The same state requires at least $25,000 in property damage liability coverage, which covers the cost of the vehicle you hit.

Considering the cost of some new cars, the $25,000 in property damage may not be enough coverage. You should check with your insurance agent for cost of additional coverage.

Liability insurance is the minimum required. This however, does NOT cover your car!

To cover your car, you need collision and comprehensive.

Collision coverage: Pays for damage to your car regardless of who caused an accident. The company must pay for the repair or up to the actual cash value of your vehicle, minus your deductible.

Comprehensive coverage (physical damage other than collision): Pays for damage to or loss of your automobile from causes other than accidents. These include hail, vandalism, flood, fire, and theft.

Most drivers will carry liability, collision and comprehensive. Especially on a new car or if you live in a hail, hurricane, flood or tornado region.

There does come a point where carrying collision and comprehensive is not cost effective. If your car is very old, you can check the blue book value, and see if the cost of carrying this coverage is worth it. Talk with your insurance agent.

The cost of your insurance will also depend on your deductible. A low deductible will obviously cost more than a high deductible. Your insurance agent can run the numbers with you. Deductible is what you pay out of pocket when you file a claim for whatever reason.

Even though insurance or financial responsibility is required in every state, there are still many people that will get the insurance just for when they get it registered, then let it drop. Then you will need:

Uninsured/underinsured motorist (UM/UIM) coverage: Pays for your injuries and property damage caused by a hit-and-run driver or a motorist without liability insurance. It will also pay when your medical and car repair bills are higher than the other driver's liability coverage.

One other insurance coverage to consider is GAP insurance. This pays the difference between the actual cash value of a vehicle and the amount still to be paid on the loan. Some gap policies may also cover the amount of the deductible. If you buy a brand new car, or you owe more on your loan then what the car is worth, you might consider this coverage. If you are in an accident, the insurance company will only pay their value on the car. If you still owe more than that on your loan, you are responsible for the difference.

Make an appointment to visit your insurance agent, with or without your parents. They can help you understand the terms, and show you the difference in cost for your insurance. There is no specific dedicated age that a child has to be removed from their parents insurance. The longer you can stay on your parents insurance, the cheaper it is going to be for you.

Happy Car Hunting!!

Don't let someone's bright idea dim your own.
~ Anonymous

Chapter 9 Worksheets

Buying a Car

How much car can you afford?

Exercise 1

Check your newspaper, find the car you want.

Go to: www.edmunds.com. (Edmunds is always updating their website, so you may have to work around these next instructions to find your answers).

Scroll down to 'New Cars', Calculators, and click.

Then click on 'Monthly Loan Payment', Select a vehicle. A screen should come up for you to plug in in your car.

Plug in the car you'd like and find out what it should be costing in our area. For example – a 2007 Honda Accord, 4 door sedan, on the day that I checked, was $11,136 plus the tax, title and registration of $919 + 167.

Check your newspaper, can you find the car you want for the price that Edmunds.com says it should cost?
What type of car do you want? _____
What year? _____
How much does it cost? _____
Click on next to continue to your monthly payment.
You can guess on your interest rate. Right now car loan interest rates are really good – so plug in 3%. (Remember – if your credit is NOT good – you will be paying a much higher interest rate).
What would your monthly payments be? _____

Part 2

How much would the insurance be on this car? Call your insurance people and have a little chat. You might explain you're doing a school project. Ask them for an estimate on the car. If you are on your parents insurance, find out who they are and give them a call. They'll be happy to make a guesstimate for you!
So how much would your insurance cost? $_____

Is this paid monthly? Or every 6 months? You'll probably find that if you pay every 6 months, it will be a little cheaper – most insurance company's charge a monthly processing fee. On my insurance – it is $3.50 a month. That can really add up. So which way will be cheaper for you?

What will your insurance go down to once you turn 25 years old? $_____

How much will it go up if you're on your own policy?
$_____

Exercise 2

Now – take a look at a new car. Pick your dream car and go through this process again.

Go back to http://www.edmunds.com/ and plug in your dream car.

What kind of car is it? _____

What year? _____

How much does it cost? _____ Plus tax, title and registration = $_____ total cost.

How much will your monthly payments be? $_____

Don't forget, your insurance will also go up for a newer model car. Be sure you check with you insurance people before you buy the car!!

Exercise 3

Call or go to your bank or credit union and speak to a loan officer. Ask them what is the <u>oldest</u> a car can be for them to still finance it.

Many lenders will not lend on a car more than 10 years old, if they do, the time is short, like 36 months, or the loan rate will be increased, or both. So check with your lender.

What insurance do they require while there is still a loan on the car? Comprehensive or just liability?

_____

What insurance do you need when the loan is paid off? _____

Discuss with your insurance people what the differences are between comprehensive and liability and when do they recommend just liability.

Chapter 10 – Buying a House

Learning Objectives: At the completion of this chapter, the student is expected to:

1. Analyze costs and benefits of owning versus renting housing.
2. Develop a short-term saving strategy to achieve a goal such as establishing and maintaining an emergency fund.
3. Examine the components of the cost of borrowing, including annual percentage rate (APR), fixed versus variable interest, length of term, grace period, and additional fees such as late payment, cash advance, and prepayment penalties.
4. Explain strategies to reduce total cost of borrowing such as making a higher down payment and additional principal payments.
5. Explain the costs and benefits of property insurance, including homeowner's and renter's insurance;

Uses mathematical processes to:

1. Use technology to create amortization models to investigate home financing and compare buying a home to renting a home.

Chapter Ten

House Buying and Mortgages

As I write this section, we are coming out of the recession when foreclosures were an all-time high since the 1930s recession. In some states, 1 of 6 people received a foreclosure notice and were losing their homes back to the mortgage lender. The economy is still pretty tough, but there are many different reasons why someone could lose their house. For a lot of people during the recession, they lost their jobs and couldn't make their payments. But, even when we're not in a recession, some people lose their homes from bad planning, greed, and stupidity. You may say that stupidity is a harsh word for these poor people losing their houses, but let's go back to my basic saying of "no one cares more about your money than you do." Many of these people "trusted" their real estate agent, or even their bank. Once again, who are they working for? Ok, so I'll come back to this.

Let us begin with some basics. When you are looking for a house, what are you looking for? (Homework again!) What you want and what you can afford – are usually two different things. No offense folks, but most of my generation agrees that your generation want what we have, what we have worked for over the last 35 years, *now*. In other words, for some bizarre reason, you think you are entitled to have the big house, the big TV, the expensive cars, the eating out budget – all things that took us 35 years to acquire – you want now. Having what we have takes time. Some of you may have inherited some of these things, or a large sum of money that would allow you to have all these things now, but most of you will just have to budget and take some time building your wealth and assets along the way.

When you are figuring out how much you can afford for a house, there are many different things to consider. So, the basics first. Can you tell me what PITI means? PITI is pronounced "pity." It stands for **Principal** (the amount you borrow), **Interest** (on what you borrowed), **Taxes** (property) and **Insurance** (property). How about ARM? What does that stand for? **Adjustable Rate Mortgage**. That means that your interest payment may fluctuate – either up or down according to the federal lending rate to the banks or mortgage companies. The ARM is where many people got caught in the foreclosure mess we were in. The lenders lent them money at a very, very low interest rate that would change in a year or two, maybe three. Then it would "adjust" *up* to where it should have been to begin with. People's payments would go from say $1800 a month to $2500 month. That is a difference of $700 a month. How many of us have a spare $700 month lying around?

This practice allowed many people to buy a house that they would not normally had been able to qualify for, only to lose it later. When you qualify for a home, the lender will take your income, figure all your bills, and tell you what amount payment they think you can afford, and then based on a certain percentage point, you could afford XXX amount of house. They have all these formulas for figuring out how much house you can buy. So while the person in the above example could afford a payment of $1800 they never would have qualified for a payment of $2500. This means they get their house, the all American dream, planning on being able to come up with the money later to make up the difference. What was going on in your life that you thought in 3 years you'd be able to come up with an extra $700 month to make the payment? Finishing college? Getting a raise? That would have to be some raise!! Getting married and having your spouse make up the difference? The divorce rate is over 50% - you could get married and divorced in three years' time!! OR – did you just listen to the bank or agent when they said, "oh don't worry, you'll figure it out." Now that's stupid. Remember again, who cares the most about your money? You need to think these things through. You cannot just make that type of commitment and investment without thinking about the future.

Don't get me wrong, I am not down on all ARM's. They are not all the same. Some work exactly the way they are supposed to. You start at a normal rate, which fluctuates up or down according to the federal lending rate. I know of one case where, since the federal lending rate has gone down, down, down, so has their payment. They love it, who wouldn't?

Let's go back to the normal, non-adjustable rate mortgages. Say you go to the bank, and based on your calculations and your budget, you tell the bank you can afford $1000 payment. They look over all your info and agree they will loan you $100,000 to buy a house at 6.5% interest. They tell you that your PI (principal and interest) would be $632.07 per month. You say, "Hey, wait a minute, I said I could afford $1000 and you agreed. Why can't I have $150,000? PI for that house would be $948.10" (I see you did your homework and checked an amortization calculator on the internet!). The lender says, "Oh, I'm sorry, I didn't realize you had an undisclosed income that will cover the taxes and insurance (TI)." And you look at the lender with a blank stare on your face and go "huh?"

Taxes and insurance are above and beyond the principal and interest you will be paying. If you have a loan on a house, you are required to carry insurance in case of fire and what not. The lender needs their investment protected, and so do you. Depending on where you live, the taxes and insurance can be significantly different around the country. Are you in a flood zone? Tornado Alley? Hurricane Zones? San Francisco fault line? Or in an area that is considered relatively safe? You need to find out how much insurance would cost on the house you want to buy. Let's say, based on $100,000, your insurance would be $1200 year. That breaks down to $100 a month that you need to pay, typically to the mortgage lender.

This brings us to escrow. Escrow is the amount of money you pay to the lender that *they* save for you throughout the year, in order to pay the bill for the taxes and the insurance when they are due. Insurance dates will change, but most property taxes are due at the end of the year, or by the last day of January the next year. This is where the PITI comes in. This way of paying, ensures the lender that the insurance and taxes will be paid every year.

Moving on to taxes, and hopefully you'll see how this all starts to fall together! Every house has some type of property tax. And again, depending on where you live in the country, which state, and even which city and county, taxes fluctuate from very high to very low. You need to find out what the taxes are going to be on the house you want to buy. Typically the real estate agent can get that information for you, and for sure the lender will have that info, but before you even go through the paperwork to buy a house, you should have the figure in front of you. You may ask why? Well, I'll tell you.

This is another bill that will be divided out to a monthly payment that the lender will collect from you to pay at the time the bill is due. So, let's say on that $100,000 house you want to buy, taxes will be $2200 per year. (Please keep in mind, I have no idea what the taxes would be on a house in your area. The figures I use for these calculations are guess-timates based on where I live). $2200/ year divides out to $183.33 a month. The bank would probably round that up to maybe $190 or even $200.

Now, your $100,000 house you want to buy, your monthly payment would be PI+T+I or $632.07 + $200+ $100 = $932.07 per month total house payment. There you go. Not much left over to get to your $1000 month budgeted payment you said you could afford.

So now you think you're good for the next 30 years, right? Wrong. Here's the next twist to buying a house. Land and houses generally increase in value. This is good because when it goes up in value, your equity in the house increases, giving you a better value for your dollar. Take the $100,000 house you bought. Three years later, the values in your area may have gone up, so your house is now worth $115,000. That means you have $15,000 equity in your home. (During this past recession, house values plummeted in some areas). The downside of this is that now you have to pay *taxes* on that $115,000 and probably pay a greater insurance bill because now you are covering $115,000 instead of just $100,000. Let's just say your taxes and insurance have gone up $15 a month each, $30 total. Add that to your $932.07, and your now making monthly payments of $962.07. That's even closer to your original budgeted amount of $1000 month. And folks, this continues to happen over and over. If the property values go up, the lender will pass along the increase in taxes and insurance to you and you must make the payment change.

Many people are under the misconception that once your house is paid for, you cannot lose it. Nope, Wrong. Even when it is totally paid for, you must still pay your property taxes, or the taxing agent will foreclose and take your house away to pay the back taxes. For instance, when I bought the house I live in my PITI was around $467 month – total payment. The *value* of the house is nearly tripled from when I bought it. Today, I must *save* around $350 month *just* to pay taxes and insurance (my original mortgage is paid). So, you need to keep that in mind when you buy your house – the long term effect on your pocketbook. If your $100,000 only doubles, your taxes and insurance may also double. So, instead of a $300 escrow payment, it is now $600. That's a pretty significant increase in a budget.

Before I go on to repairs, I want to make two points. Be sure you compare lenders. Your real estate person might have a mortgage lender they like to use and suggest you talk to them. That's fine. But you should compare them to your bank or credit union and see if they can help you. You will have 'closing costs' that you will be charged when you 'close' or 'buy' your house, and other than interest rates potentially being different between lenders, their closing costs could be different also. Closing costs are something you might be able to negotiate with the seller on, they might offer to pay X amount of closing costs for you, or you might ask for X amount of dollars you'd like them to pay in your offer. Your lender is required to disclose an estimated 'closing' cost sheet before you go to close on your house. Feel free to ask them about each of the charges on the sheet. And, depending on the state you live in, some of the closing costs can be run into your loan, or you have to pay them, have the cash up front for them. They will tell you how much you need to bring to closing and if it needs to be a certified or bank check, or if you can bring a personal check. Be sure and ask if they don't tell you.

Repairs

Repairs are the next twist in buying a house. When you are renting, what do you do when something breaks? I guess the answer would be based on how handy you might be, or your dad, a friend maybe, or perhaps you just call the landlord like most others do. The dishwasher breaks, call the landlord. The hot water heater is leaking, call the landlord. The house needs to be painted, call the landlord. Who are you going to call when you own a house? That's right, the plumber (or dad, or friend). And, are you ready? Who's going to pay for it? YOU!! That's right, you are. And, out of personal experience, houses are like cars. When do they break? The day after the warranty runs out, right? Exactly. So, you close on your house, and two months later, the hot water heater starts to leak. Just to buy a hot water heater, at least $400 (plus tax). Can you or someone install it? No? Call the plumber. How much is he/she going to charge? Depends on where you live and how much they get paid per hour. Guessing, I would say no less than around $150. So I hope you have a spare $550 lying around ($400 for the hot water heater and $150 for the plumber).

What about the heating and air conditioning breaking in your house. Do you need it replaced? You're looking at at least $5000. Now I know you have that kind of money lying around, right?

When you buy a house you must, must, must, set money aside for repairs, because you are in charge of that, you ARE the landlord. The money is coming out of your pocket. How long will you go with cold water? How about no heat or air conditioning? Not too long in the winter with no heat, or it will bust the water pipes. Oh, it just keeps getting worse. You need to have this saving element in your budget too. This is another item you must think about before you buy a house. This is a "don't be stupid" spot. You need to plan for these things and be ready for them. You cannot live comfortably without savings for such emergencies.

And listen, since we're talking about repairs. Let's talk a minute about a home inspection before you even buy the house. In most cases, emphasis on 'most' – in most cases, you can get a home inspection done on the house before you buy the house. Even if you are buying a house in an 'as is' condition, you can still get an inspection so you can really see what you are buying. You might be willing to buy it 'as is' – as long as you *know* what the 'as is' is.

Most of the time, a home inspection will come *after* you've put in an offer and it has been accepted by the seller. You'll have marked the contract that the deal will be conditional on the home inspection. Sometimes a dollar amount will be involved, like the seller will agree to pay x amount of money towards repairs. If the inspection reveals x amount of repairs need to be done, and the seller does the repairs, you will be buying the house. If the inspection reveals many problems, you will have the option of paying the difference yourself, or back out of the deal.

One of the most important aspects of all this is the home inspector themselves. Be sure to ask around, ask friends who they used, check references, make sure they are licensed.

Length of Loan

All right, one more item I want you to be aware of when buying a house. Time. Most lenders and agents *assume* you want your house loan for 30 years. 30 years is kind-of the norm or standard time factor. But when *borrowing* money that you are paying interest on, time is your enemy. Let's look at some examples.

Remember that $100,000 house you bought for 6.5%, 30 years? Your payment is $632.07 that covers the principal and the interest for 360 payments (12 months times 30 years). Your total interest paid *on top of* the principal is $127,544.49. I swear I just heard you go whoaaaa, that's more than double the price of the house! Exactly, it is. That's how interest works. Remember the chapter on compounding interest? Same principal, except you're doing the 'paying' instead of the receiving. In this case, the bank is the 'receiver'.

Do you want another shocker? The amount of interest paid in the first 5 years of your payments is $31,534. The amount of *principal* paid in the first 5 years is $6389. Doesn't look like a great ratio.

Now, this is where your homework comes in before you buy a house. You need to play around with an amortization calculator on the internet. And here's why. Let's take your $100,000 loan and look at it for 25 years, instead of 30. Your PI goes to $675.21 a month – just $43 more a month in your payment. But, your *total interest* payment for the 25 years goes down to $102,562. That is nearly a $25,000 savings in interest. That's a big savings. Your interest paid for the first 5 years is $31,071, but your principal payment *increases* to $9437. The interest paid in this scenario is close to the same as the amount in the 30 year note, but you paying more than $3000 extra in principal payment – which also increases your equity faster. So, you need to play with the figures. Going from 30 to 25 years is just a small increase in your payment, but you save a significant amount of interest over the life of the loan.

If you are not comfortable in a straight increase in your monthly payment, you can apply money directly to the principal amount above and beyond your regular monthly payment, regardless of which year loan you choose. Say you think you can put an extra $25 month on the principal. Just that $25 per month that you put on principal *reduces* the total interest paid by just under $16,000 and reduces the length of the loan by 3.17 years. WOW! Just $25 a month more. $50 a month extra saves you nearly $28,000 in interest and shortens the length of your loan by about 5 1/2 years. What a savings!!! Maybe you get a bonus at work that you can put on it once a year, maybe you can put $500 from your tax return, or maybe you get a raise at work. How about one extra payment a year? If you do it starting at year one, it will reduce your loan by 4 years. Just one extra payment saves you about $19,000 in interest. It all adds up. As long as you keep making your regular payment, it will go on the principal balance, reducing your interest and length of time you have to pay for the house. If I could save $16,000 by paying $25 extra a month, I would definitely do it when I could! One caveat here, make sure when you make the extra payments, it does go on your principal.

I did notice on a loan that we paid off early, that if the extra payment was not made at the time of the payment, they took whatever interest had accrued since the last payment out first, and then applied the rest to the principal. This works out ok too, because when you make your next payment, less goes to the interest and more to the principal anyway. So try and send the extra when you make your payment, and designate that money for the principal. Ok?

So, play with the amortization calculators on the internet. Talk with your lender. Make sure there are no pre-payment penalties. Save your emergency money, and enjoy the home you can afford today, not one you hope you can afford in 3 years. Your payment amount will go up, even with a set percentage loan rate. Be prepared by buying what you can afford now. Don't let *anyone* talk you into a house that does not fit your budget, including your spouse. Life is stressful enough without worrying about a house payment, repairs and increases!!

Interest Only Loans

One more thought to wrap up this chapter: interest only loans. My personal opinion on those types of loans is run, don't walk, away from them. Again, my personal opinion. In order to buy a house you can't really afford in the first place, you agree to pay an interest only loan for 5 – 7 years, with an option then to amortize the balance of the loan over the next 25 years. So you make an interest only payment for 5 years on the house you are living in, and what do you have?? Nothing. Because you have not made any payment on the principal! Once your 5 year plan is up, you still have the original principal payment, which will now be higher because you have gone to a 25 year plan. Get it?

Let me give you an example. Say you *just can't live* without that $200,000 house you've seen. But, money's kind of tight. You still have only a budget of $1000 per month. The real estate agent says "no problem, we'll figure something out. We will GET you THAT house!! No matter what it takes. YOU deserve it!!" WOW, what a great person!!! So they come back and say, "I've got a lender that will get you in that house, on budget, with a 5 year interest only loan. You've got your house!!" squeal, squeal, jump up and down yeahhh! I've got my house. Where do I sign?

You'd better be careful what you sign. First, your interest only loan for the next 5 years is $1083.33. Only $83.33 over your stated budget. Surely you can come up with that!! No problem, right? You will make 60 monthly payments of $1,083.33, then 300 (25 years x 12) monthly payments of $1,350.41. Uh oh. Now you are over your budget by $350.41. And, did you forget your taxes and insurance that you will still have to be paying? The total price you will pay for that house is $470,126.09. $270,126.09 is interest. This is a HUGE red flag for me. If you can't afford the principal payment now, what makes you think it will be better in 5 years? What if you lose your job? Marry, divorce, remarry? Kids need braces? Better to be in a house you can afford, than one you *hope* you can afford in 5 years. Think about it folks.

Read what you sign, and understand it. If you don't understand it, ASK. That's how we learn. Do the research, check the prices, and be realistic about what you can afford. Hey, if you get a great raise in 5 years, or a new job, then move to a bigger house if you want, but right now, buy what you can afford.

Homeowners and Renters Insurance

A home is a large and expensive purchase that you want to protect. Most people, though not all, will carry homeowners insurance.

If you owe a mortgage on the house, you are required to carry insurance. This protects the lender if something were to happen, ie: tornado, fire, hurricane, etc. If your home is destroyed, you will be able to rebuild or repair it. Without insurance, this money needs to come out of your pocket. Most people do not have that much spare cash lying around. The house acts as collateral for the loan, and the lender wants their property protected.

When you do not owe a lender any longer, you have paid off the house, you technically/ legally are not required to carry homeowners insurance. However, if something happens to the house, you have to be able to repair, replace, or rebuild the house with your savings. Again, most people do not have that kind of money lying around.

Homeowners insurance helps you replace your things. If your property is destroyed or your house is robbed and everything is stolen, your homeowner's insurance policy will pay for you to replace all of the things- from your bed to your silverware- that you keep inside the house.
Most homeowner policies will also pay for you to have a place to live while your home is being repaired.

Homeowners insurance also protects you from lawsuits. If someone comes to your house and is injured on your property, you can be sued. Homeowners insurance will pay legal bills and any damages awarded to the injured party, up to the limits of your policy.
Your insurance company generally sets the amount your house will be insured for. This usually is their guesstimate as to the entire cost of rebuilding and replacing everything. If you think the amount is too high or too low, you need to speak to your agent.

Additionally, you may have 'riders' on your policy. If you have furs, jewelry, antiques, etc, you could add additional coverage for these items on your policy to be sure they are covered completely.

It would be helpful to take pictures in each room, open doors and drawers and take a snapshot to be stored in a safe place, for proof if something happens, and to help you remember everything you have.

Today, you can keep copies in a safe deposit box, on a flash drive with a few family members, or even just the cloud now. It would be difficult to remember everything you have during a trauma like a fire.

Renters Insurance

When you are a renter, your belongings are not covered by the landlord policy. Their policy covers the building. Their policy does not cover your possessions, so you have to do this on your own.

Renters Insurance is a type of insurance that covers your belongings against fire, theft, tornado, etc. while you are renting.

It usually also provides personal liability coverage and additional living expenses if you need to live elsewhere while your rent is being repaired. Possessions can be covered for their replacement cost or the actual cash value, which includes depreciation. Be sure you make a good list and a good estimate for your insurance agent, including the antiques, jewelry, computers, tvs, etc.

It would be helpful to take pictures in each room, open doors and drawers and take a snapshot to be stored in a safe place, for proof is something happens, and to help you remember everything you have. Today, you can keep copies in a safe deposit box, on a flash drive with a few family members, or even just a cloud now. It would be difficult to remember everything you have during a trauma like a fire.

It is not expensive. One policy I priced was for $28,000 coverage for about $180.00 a year. Totally worth it!!

Happy House Buying!!!

When your heart is in your dream, no request is too extreme.
~ Jiminy Cricket

Chapter 10 Worksheets

House Buying and Mortgages

What kind of a house (single family, condo, townhouse) do you want? How many bedrooms, bathrooms, how big? 1200 sq feet, 1700 sq feet, 2500 sq feet? How big does your starter home need to be?

In the Sunday paper, in the house section, find a house that you think you might like. Some will tell you how big they are, most will tell you how many bedrooms and bathrooms. A 3/2/1 is a 3 bedroom, 2 bath, 1 car garage.

Find one that might fit your 'wants' and write down how much that house costs. $_____

Now – go to http://www.amortization-schedule.info/

Fill in the cost of the house and let's play around with the years. (You'll find 'total interest paid' on the bottom of the page.) If this site is not working, just google 'amortization schedule' and one should come up. Use 6% for your interest rate. If your credit is bad, your interest rate will be higher. If your credit is good, your interest rate will be less.

30 years mortgage:

Cost of house $_____

Monthly **PI** (principal and interest) payment would be $_____

Total amount of interest paid over the life of the loan $_____

Total cost house + interest $_____

Now – add in 'guesstimate' **T**axes and **I**nsurance.

For every $100,000 add in $1100 year for Insurance and $2000 year for Taxes. Add together and divide by 12 (months) and add that to your monthly PI payment. (For example: if you want a $200,000 house – $1100 x 2 = $2200. $2000 x 2= $4000. $2200 + 4000 = $6200.

$6200 / 12 = $517 (rounded up). Add $517 to your PI.)

How much is your monthly payment now? $_____   Can you still afford it?

Let's keep playing:

Change your mortgage years to **25** and run this again.

Cost of house $_____

Monthly PI payment $_____

Total interest paid over the life of the loan $_____

Total cost house + interest $_____

Add in your taxes and insurance and your new monthly payment is $_____.

How much of a difference is the new monthly payment between 30 and 25 years? _____.

How much interest would you save by going to 25 years instead of 30? $_____.

20 years mortgage?

Cost of house $_____

Monthly PI payment $_____

Total interest paid over the life of the loan $_____

Total cost house + interest $_____

Add in your taxes and insurance and your new monthly payment is $_____.
How much of a difference is the new monthly payment between 30 and 20 years? _____.

How much interest would you save by going to 20 years instead of 30? $_____.

15 year mortgage?

Cost of house $_____

Monthly PI payment $_____

Total interest paid over the life of the loan $_____

Total cost house + interest $_____

Add in your taxes and insurance and your new monthly payment is $_____

How much of a difference is the new monthly payment between 30 and 15 years? _____

How much interest would you save by going to 15 years instead of 30? $_____

Change the 'Payment Frequency' to bi-weekly. This means that you would be paying your mortgage every 2 weeks. Change the 'years' back to whichever one you think you can afford, and run this again.

What does this do to your payment? _____

Add in taxes and insurance and your new monthly payment would be $_____

How much interest would you now be paying? _____

Can you afford this house?

PMI

Keep in mind, many financial advisors recommend you have a 20% down payment. How much do you need? $_____

Most people only have 5% or 10% down. But if you put down 20%, then you don't have to pay PMI – Private Mortgage Insurance. PMI is extra insurance that lenders require from homebuyers who obtain loans that are more than 80% of their new home's value. In other words, buyers with less than a 20% down payment are normally required to pay PMI.

Under *The Homeowner's Protection Act (HPA) of 1998*, if you have a good pay history and your loan is now 80% of loan or appraisal value, you can request the PMI to be cancelled.

PMI typically costs between 0.5% to 1% of the entire loan amount on an annual basis. On a $100,000 loan this means the homeowner could be paying as much as $1,000 a year, or $83.33 per month - assuming a 1% PMI fee.

Based on 1% PMI, if you put down 10%, how much will be added to your monthly payment to cover the PMI? $_____

Also, rule of thumb is you need to be able to save 1% of the value of the house, per year, for repairs. So if the house is $100,000 – you need to be saving $1000 for repairs, or $83.33 per month.

This is **in addition to** your emergency fund!! Don't confuse the two!!

Keep in mind, that your <u>total</u> housing expense should only be 35% of your income. So if you are making $2000, your housing should not exceed $700, including saving for repairs! (No wonder it takes 2 incomes!!) Now, how much house can you afford to buy??

Chapter 11- Insurance and Wills

Learning Objectives: At the completion of this chapter, the student is expected to:

1. Identify benefits such life insurance, and disability insurance.
2. Identify costs of retirement such as living expenses, health care expenses, and long-term care expenses.
3. Define insurance terminology, including premiums, deductibles, co-pays, and policy limits.
4. Explain the costs and benefits of disability and long-term care insurance.
5. Explain the costs and benefits of life insurance, including term insurance and whole life insurance.
6. Understand the importance of guardianship of minor children through insurance, wills, and beneficiary designation.

Uses mathematical processes to:

1. Analyze and compare coverage options and rates in insurance.

Chapter Eleven

INSURANCE & WILLS

Life insurance is an insurance policy that is paid to beneficiaries upon death of the insured. This provides an influx of cash for the surviving family so they can pay for funeral expenses, medical bills, perhaps pay off the mortgage, and provide for the family financially.

Generally, a single or an old person does not necessarily need life insurance. If they have sufficient funds in an account to cover funeral expenses and the medical bills, a life insurance policy is not needed. An 18 year old or an 80 year old women who has no dependents, generally does not need to have life insurance. A little money in the bank to bury or cremate them is all they need. However, if you have a family, especially if you are the main money provider for the family, how is your family going to take care of themselves if you die? As soon as you start a family, you need to have a life insurance policy. Taking care of your loved ones is the main purpose to have life insurance.

Life Insurance – Whole and Term

Term Life Insurance

Term life is a policy that covers an individual (the insured) for a set period of time. Typically, term life is available in 10, 15, 20 and 30 year term lengths. Term life lasts for the term of the policy. Once the policy expires, the insured may be able to renew the policy on an annual basis or for the next 10 or 20 years. This will vary by company.

Term Insurance is the best life insurance product for its simplicity and cheapness. It gives you a lump sum amount in case of death and has no clauses and conditions. It's very simple to understand and the cheapest insurance product as well.

Life insurance is not an investment. This is to replace the income you would make if you were alive, not create income.

Term life insurance can be very inexpensive depending on your age, your health, and whether you smoke or not. For non-smokers, doing a quick check, I found prices for a 20 year old male, non-smoker, no exam needed, a policy good for 20 years, $250,000 for only $13 a month. For $500,000 coverage, $20 a month. For $1 million, $33 a month.

If they were a smoker, they would be paying $103 a month for $1 million.

A 50 year old male, non-smoker, who still has 15 to 20 years of earning power left, using the 20 year term, they would pay $41 for $250,000, $75 for $500,000 and $143 for $1 million.
You can see that when your first term life has expired, you can expect to pay more for your insurance.

Whole life insurance

Whole life insurance is also called continuous premium whole life insurance, ordinary life insurance, permanent life insurance, or straight life insurance.
A whole life insurance policy is a contract between the insured and the insurer to pay a fixed amount upon death. The premiums are generally fixed for life.

Like all permanent life insurance policies, whole life provides lifelong coverage and includes an investment component known as the policy's cash value. The cash value grows slowly, tax-deferred, meaning you won't pay taxes on its gains while they're accumulating.

The cash value account is one reason whole life insurance premiums are higher than premiums for term insurance. Cash value grows slowly at first and generally picks up speed after several years.

You can borrow money against the account or surrender the policy for the cash. But if you don't repay policy loans with interest, you'll reduce your death benefit, and if you surrender the policy, you'll no longer have coverage.

Once you have accumulated enough cash value, you can opt to use it to cover your premium payments. This is known as being "paid up." If you decide to withdraw some cash value, you may have to resume premium payments to keep the life insurance policy in force.

Whole life is more expensive than term life. For a 30 year old male, one chart shows $250,000 coverage (again – this is for life) would cost $2385 a year. The same shows that for 30 year term, the same 30 year old male would be paying $240 a year. Again – keep in mind, that this term price will go up once they have to renew.

Do not let the idea of withdrawing from your life insurance policy sway you. You MUST understand how withdrawing the cash will affect your policy. Additionally, there are several well-known financial advisors that are completely opposed to whole life terms for being too expensive, too complicated, and stating that the cash value that you can take out is never close to the amount of the money that you invest annually. Also, that if you took the difference between the term life cost vs the whole life cost and invested that yourself (Roth IRA), you would have a much higher value on your money.

One more point…if the value on your $500,000 policy, for example, actually has a cash value of say $650,000, your family is still only going to get the $500,000. The cash value goes to the insurer and they pay only the agreed upon contract.

Beneficiaries and Divorce

When / if you divorce, remember to change your beneficiaries on your life insurance policy, your banking documents, your 401k, pension, Roth IRA – and any other form of policy where you have designated a beneficiary.

There are many instances where this is forgotten, you die, and your ex-spouse gets the money! You do NOT want this to happen. Your new spouse will have no basis to argue and get the policy.

Disability Insurance

Disability insurance is a policy, long term or short term, which covers loss of income during this time. Short term is considered up to a year, where long term is considered from a few years to the rest of your life.

Many jobs will offer disability insurance as an option to their employment package where others do not and you need to take it out on your own.

Your ability to earn an income is considered an asset. Insuring this asset is a practice that, according to some 2015 figures, only 31% of the population actually has. If you cannot replace your income from savings for an extended period of time, they encourage you to have disability insurance in case some injury (broken leg, back injury) or illness (cancer, heart attacks) happens.

Short term disability insurance generally replaces 60% – 70% of your base salary with a monthly cap. There may be a waiting period of up to two weeks after you become disabled before the benefits begin.

Long term disability insurance generally replaces 40% - 60% of your base salary with a monthly cap. If you remain disabled, benefits may end after a specified number of years or last until you reach retirement age, depending on the policy.

Premiums generally cost between 1% and 3% of your annual income. However, there are several factors that will affect the cost, including, but not limited to, your age, male or female, your job – high risk or not, smoking, your income, and extra benefits like job training.

Long Term Care Insurance

Long term care insurance is a policy that will help pay for any long term care you might need, like a nursing home or in home care.

Individuals who require long-term care are generally not sick in the traditional sense, but instead, are unable to perform two of the six activities of daily life such as dressing, bathing, eating, toileting, continence, transferring (getting in and out of a bed or chair), and walking.

Age for needing long term care is generally not an issue. About 40% of those receiving long term care are between the ages of 18 and 65. They estimate that 70% of the population over age 65 will need long term care at some point in their lives.

Long-term care insurance generally covers home care, assisted living, adult daycare, respite care, hospice care, nursing home and Alzheimer's facilities. If your policy allows, it will pay for a visiting or live-in caregiver, companion, housekeeper, therapist or private duty nurse up to seven days a week, 24 hours a day (up to the policy benefit maximum).

Most people do not carry a long term care policy as they can be expensive. Quotes for a healthy 60 year old couple (discount included for covering both people) ranges from $2600 to $5000 a year, with limits on total payout.

Opinion varies on whether you should or shouldn't buy long term care insurance. If you come from a relatively healthy household (your mom is 88 and still living at home), then you might not buy it. Rates are rising faster than inflation, so even if you can afford it now, can you later? Many companies that were once in business selling long term care policies are now out of business – along with the money you've already spent. If you have children that can help with a few of the chores or be there for a recovery, then most will say you don't need it. However, if you've seen your folks at a young age with Alzheimer's or dementia at a young age living in a nursing home or assisted facility, then you might should consider it.

There are many options to choose from when you consider your policy. Do your research and speak to a reputable agent.

<u>Wills</u>

A will is a legal document that states your wishes upon your death. There are two main reasons why you would have a will. First, the disposition of your property, who you want to get what you own; and second, naming a legal guardian for your minor children. You will also name an executor, the person in charge of executing your will.

There is no exact age as to when you should create a will. Most young people never even think about having a will. Most young people do not have enough property to worry about what happens to it. If you have very specific items you want someone specifically to get, you could just make a note on the bottom of it.

Most young people never even think about dying. However, it is a reality and there does come a time when you should have a will.

Once you become a parent, it is really important to have a will, if only to designate a guardian for your child/children. You need to speak to the people whom you are considering to see if they would raise your children. No, not all are going to jump at the chance of taking in and raising the kiddos. Common guardians include your parents, brothers or sisters, other family members, or best friends. Keep in mind your parents are aging, your brothers and sisters may be in school, best friends may already have 4 children. Do they have the financial capability – especially if you did NOT get a term life insurance policy to help with expenses? Would they need to move to a larger house? Would they love them like their own? And, if you choose best friends over parents, you need to let your parents know (hopefully) when you make that choice. You don't want them assuming they would be getting your children and then get blindsided when they don't.

Keep in mind, if you marry, have children and divorce, your ex-spouse will automatically get custody of the child/children. There is not much you can do about that. If you are a single parent without the other parent in the picture, but their name is on the birth certificate, you must have a guardian listed for the child and certainly visit with a family attorney because the other 'parent' could make claim on your child at that point. This is where it gets messy and definitely see an attorney.

When you buy a house is another reason to get a will. Who gets the house if you die? If you live in a community property state, the spouse, if all has been amicable, generally gets the house and all other property you acquired together. In a separate property state, the spouse is not automatically entitled to half the interest in all property acquired since the marriage. You need to do a little research and speak with an attorney.

Wills do not have to be complicated. You can even download and fill one in from the internet, then just have it notarized. But once you have children, if relations are complicated, you need to consult with an attorney. Perhaps your town has a free or cheap legal clinic in town.

Probate

Probate is the legal process where a will is "proved" in a court and accepted as a valid public document that is the true last testament of the deceased. Probate can tie up a person's property up in court for months if not years. You may or may not need an attorney to get the paperwork done and filed on schedule. Most of this is just procedure to process the will, but probate can give creditors claim or other family members' time to contest the will. Some states allow some property to pass through without probate, while others require probate unless the property is in a revocable living trust, or joint tenancy.

Joint tenancy is when you own property with someone, there is simply a check box on the form, like a deed, stating you want to hold this property in joint tenancy – usually with your spouse. This property will also avoid probate.

Living trusts were created to let people make a legal way around probate. The advantage of holding your valuable property in trust is that after your death, the trust property is not part of your probate estate. That's because a trustee -- not you as an individual -- owns the trust property. After your death, the trustee can easily and quickly transfer the trust property to the family or friends you left it to, without probate. You specify in the trust document who you want to inherit the property.

Most people want to avoid probate at all costs. Speak with an attorney!

Even if you don't have or need a will, you should speak to your parents about your wishes – burial or cremation. You can choose on your own what you would like after your death. It does not need to be the same as your parents. And, it can change over time. Be sure your loved ones know what you want. Additionally, your 'will' will probably change over time also. Perhaps you named a guardian and that person didn't turn out as you expected, or perhaps they died. You will need a new guardian. Perhaps you named your parents as recipients of your property, but now you have a spouse. Wills need to be kept up to date.

Die without a will

If you die without a will, you have died "intestate." When this happens, the intestacy laws of the state where you reside will determine how your property is distributed upon your death.

The *laws of intestate succession* vary greatly depending on whether you were single or married, or had children. In most cases, your property is distributed in split shares to your "heirs," which could include your surviving spouse, siblings, aunts and uncles, nieces, nephews, and distant relatives. Generally, when no relatives can be found, the entire estate goes to the state. One more reason to have a will! Someone other than the state should get your possessions, even if you have to leave it all to charity. Be sure and check the rules of your state!

Chapter 11 Assignment

Insurance and Wills

There are no worksheets for this chapter. Take time in class to discuss any questions the students might have regarding insurance and wills.

THE END

ANSWERS

Chapters 1 & 2

Compound Interest and IRA's

Exercise 1:

A. What is the answer? **$17,804.41**

B. What is the answer? **$449,346.52**
C. What is the answer? **$35,608.82**

D. What is the answer? **$898,693.03**

Exercise 2:

E. What is the answer? **$526,488.66**

F. How much of E is the original money YOU put in? **$22,000.00** (2,000+ (2k x 10 years) =

Exercise 3:

A. **$20,124.91**

B. **$863,685.80**

C. **$40,249.82**

D. **$1,727,371.61**

Exercise 4:

Student Answers will be different in this section.

What year do you expect to retire? _____

Is there a fund for that year? _____

What is the latest date fund? (ie: 2040, 2045?) _____

Look at the other target date funds. Which one is currently paying the highest interest?
_____

What is the maximum amount you could you invest annually in a Roth IRA if you had the funds? $6000.00

- Call your bank or credit union; ask them what their interest rate for a Roth IRA is. What is it? _____
- Would you make more money with an online broker or a bank/credit union? _____
- When should you start saving for retirement? _____

PLEASE KEEP IN MIND, IF YOUR BANK/CREDIT UNION SAYS 6% - THEY PROBABLY MEAN .6% OR EVEN .06%. (Unfortunately, many of the workers do not know the difference. Where I live, you will NOT find anyone in town paying more than 1.5% for a Roth IRA. I would doubt any answer much higher than that from a bank/credit union.)

Chapter 3

401K Plan
Exercise 1 Part One

So, if your salary is $50,000, how much is 6%? **$3,000.00**
($50,000 x .06)

If your employer matches 50%, how much will they put into your account? **$1500.00**   **($3000 x .50)**

If you are paid every 2 weeks, how much of that 6% will be coming out of each paycheck? **$115.38 ($3000/26)**

If your salary is $100,000 and you contribute 15% to your 401k, how much annually are you saving per year? **$15,000.00**
($100,000 x .15)

How much is your boss going to contribute? **$3,000.00**
(Remember, 50% of 6%, not 50% of 15%). **($100,000 x .06 x .50 = $3,000)**

How much needs to come out of your paycheck if you are paid monthly to contribute the 15%? **$1250.00 ($15,000 / 12 = $1250)**

Part Two

The second 'usual' way is that they will match dollar for dollar up to 5% of your annual salary.

So if your salary is $50,000, 5% of your salary is? **$2500.00**

(50,000 x .05)

How much is your boss putting in? **$2500.00 ($ for $)**

If you are paid every 2 weeks, how much will come out of each of your paychecks? **$96.15 ($2500 / 26 = $96.15)**

If you salary is $100,000 and you want to save 17%, how much are you saving per year? **$17,000.00 (100,000 x .17)**

How much is your boss putting into your retirement plan? **$5,000.00**

(Remember – match is 5% $ for $ of $100,000 (not of the $17k)).

If you are paid monthly, how much is coming out of each paycheck? **$1416.67 ($17,000/ 12)**

Exercise 2

You have been at your job for 5 years, and you have saved $80,000, and you withdraw your money. How much are you giving to the IRS? **$16,000.00 ($80,000 x .20 = $16,000)**

If you roll over your money into another qualified retirement account, how much is going to go to the IRS? **$0** And yes, the space here is tiny because the answer is 0.

Chapter 4

Budgets

Exercise 1: Create a <u>balanced</u> monthly budget based on a full time, 40 hour week minimum wage ($7.25) job. **$7.25 x 40 x 4 = $1160 - $174 (15%) = $986. If the minimum wage in your area is higher, feel free to use it.** Remember to take out 15% for the Federal taxes.

Each student budget will be different, especially if they are living at home. Have them create a hypothetical budget – as if they were NOT living at home.

	Monthly Actual Amount	Monthly Budget Amount
INCOME: WAGES YOU EARN		$986.00
$XXXX.XX		
EXPENSES:		
HOUSE: Mortgage or Rent		
Homeowners/Renters Insurance		
UTILIITES: Electricity		
Water and Sewer		
Natural Gas or Oil		
Telephone (Land Line, Cell)		
FOOD: Groceries		
Eating Out, Lunches, Snacks		
HEALTH & MEDICAL		
Insurance (medical,dental,vision)		
Unreimbursed Medical Expenses, Copays		
TRANSPORTATION:		
Car Payments		
Gasoline/Oil		
Auto Repairs/Maintenance/Fees		
Auto Insurance		
Other Transportation (tolls, bus, subway, taxis)		
DEBT PAYMENTS:		
Credit Cards		
Student Loans		
ENTERTAINMENT/RECREATION:		
Vacations		
Pets		
Clothing		
INVESTMENTS AND SAVINGS:		
401(K)or IRA		
Savings		
Emergency Fund		
MISCELLANEOUS:		
Toiletries, Household Products		
Gifts/Donations		
Grooming (Hair, Make-up, Other)		
Miscellaneous Expense		

Total Expenses		
Total Income – Total Expenses =		

Exercise 2

Create a balanced monthly budget based a full time, 40 hour week, wage ($18.00) job. Remember to take out approximately 20% for taxes. **$18. x 40 x 4 = $2880 - $576 (20%) = $2304. (It is higher here because you are making more money.)** Make sure on this one you have emergency savings and savings for retirement. **Create a hypothetical budget as if they were NOT living at home.**

	Monthly Actual Amount	Monthly Budget Amount
INCOME: WAGES YOU EARN		$2304
$XXXX.XX		
EXPENSES:		
HOUSE: Mortgage or Rent		
Homeowners/Renters Insurance		
UTILIITES: Electricity		
Water and Sewer		
Natural Gas or Oil		
Telephone (Land Line, Cell)		
FOOD: Groceries		
Eating Out, Lunches, Snacks		
HEALTH & MEDICAL		
Insurance (medical,dental,vision)		
Unreimbursed Medical Expenses, Copays		
TRANSPORTATION:		
Car Payments		
Gasoline/Oil		
Auto Repairs/Maintenance/Fees		
Auto Insurance		
Other Transportation (tolls, bus, subway, taxis)		
DEBT PAYMENTS:		
Credit Cards		
Student Loans		
ENTERTAINMENT/RECREATION:		
Vacations		
Pets		
Clothing		
INVESTMENTS AND SAVINGS:		
401(K)or IRA		

Savings		
Emergency Fund		
MISCELLANEOUS:		
Toiletries, Household Products		
Gifts/Donations		
Grooming (Hair, Make-up, Other)		
Miscellaneous Expense		
Total Expenses		
Total Income – Total Expenses =		

Was this budget easier making ends meet? _____

What did you have to change? _____

Based on these two scenarios, how much money do you think you need to make an hour in order to live the lifestyle you'd like? _____

Exercise 3

Google "Reality Check" and your state. (ie: Reality check Texas)

Student answers will be different here.

Chapter 5

Credit and Debit Cards

Exercise 1

What is the minimum payment to start? **$48.00**

How long will it take you to pay off this $2400 if you only make minimum payments? **30+ YEARS**

How much total interest are you going to waste? **$11,752.66**.

Did you have a heart attack when you saw this amount? **YES**

Was it worth it? **NO**

Part 2

How long will it take you now to pay off the $2400? **135 months 11.25 YEARS**

How much interest are you going to spend now? **$4065.70**
Go back to table and scroll down to see total interest paid.

What is the difference in time between *only* making minimum payment vs. continuing to make the $48 a month? **Approximately 29 years**

How much interest will you save? **$7,686.96**
($11,752.66. – $4065.70 = $7,686.96)

Part 3

Let's cut the time in half. Plug in 6 years **(72 months)** and hit "get monthly payment." What do you get for a monthly payment? **$60.00**

How much more a month are you going to be paying from the $48? **$12.00**

How much interest are you going to save? **$2134.13**
($4065.70- $1931.57 = $2134.13)

Plug in 5 years. **(60 months)**

What do you get for a monthly payment? **$66.00**

How much more a month do you need to pay from the 6 years? **$6.00**

Plug in 3 years, **(36 months)** now what is your monthly payment? **$91.53**

Chapter 6

Paychecks and W2 – No Worksheets

Chapter 7

Income Tax

Exercise 1

1. Are you required by law to file an income tax return? Yes or No? __NO__
   Why or why not? __I made less than the standard deduction.

2. If you are not required to file a return, why would you want to?
   ____To get all my Income Tax withheld back. _____

3. If you file a return, will you be claiming your Personal Exemption or your parents?
   __Parents_____
   Why? _Because I am their dependent _____

4. How much money would you expect to get back? ___$187___

5. How do you report the $18 dividend from you credit union?

   ____As interest _____

6. Do you get your Social Security and Medicare tax withheld back? _No___

Chapter 8

College and Financial Aid – No worksheets.

Chapter 9

Buying a Car

Student answers will be different depending on the make and model of car they work with

Chapter 10

House Buying and Mortgages

Student answers will be different for most of this section depending on the house they choose.

Based on 1% PMI, if you put down 10%, how much will be added to your monthly payment to cover the PMI? **$75.00**

($100,000 - $10,000 (down payment) = $90,000 x 1% = $900 / 12 = $75.00)

Chapter 11

Life Insurance and Wills – No Worksheets

APPENDIX

Social Studies Models

(1) Earning and spending. The student understands how to set personal financial goals. The student is expected to (Chapter 4)

    (A) differentiate between needs and wants in evaluating spending decisions;

    (B) investigate the student's money personality, including spending and saving propensity;

    (C) demonstrate an understanding of the value and benefits of charitable giving; and

    (D) develop financial goals for the short, medium, and long term that are specific, measurable, attainable, realistic, and time based.

    (E) develop a budget that incorporates short-, medium-, and long-term financial goals;

    (F) evaluate the impact of unplanned spending on a budget.

(2) Earning and spending. The student analyzes components of compensation from employment. The student is expected to: (Chapter 6, 11)

    (A) identify benefits such as health insurance contributions, retirement benefits, sick leave, vacation pay, flexible spending account, health savings account, workers compensation, life insurance, and disability insurance;

    (B) identify taxes that are deducted from paychecks, including Federal Insurance Contributions Act (FICA) and federal income taxes; and

    (C) calculate gross and net pay using information on a paycheck.

(3) Earning and spending. The student critically evaluates consumption decisions. The student is expected to: (Various Chapters throughout)

    (A) analyze costs and benefits of owning versus renting housing;

    (B) analyze costs and benefits of owning versus leasing a vehicle;

    (C) compare total costs of alternative methods of payment such as rent-to-own, store credit, installment agreements, cash, bank credit card, and debit card; and

    (D) apply strategies for making informed decisions about purchasing consumer goods such as comparing prices per unit, looking for sales or promotions, and negotiating price.

(4) Saving and investing. The student understands the importance of saving and investing in creating wealth and building assets. The student is expected to: (Chapters 2, 3, 4, 7, 10)

(A) develop a short-term saving strategy to achieve a goal such as establishing and maintaining an emergency fund;

(B) develop an intermediate-term saving and investing strategy to achieve a goal such as accumulating a down payment on a home or vehicle;

(C) explain the tax benefits of charitable contributions; and

(D) develop a long-term investing strategy to achieve a goal such as a financially secure retirement.

(5) Saving and investing. The student understands the implementation of a saving and investing plan. The student is expected to: (Chapters 1, 2, 3)

(A) discuss the role of financial institutions and markets in saving and investing;

(B) demonstrate the impact of compound growth over time;

(C) evaluate the costs and benefits of various savings options such as bank savings accounts, certificates of deposit, and money market mutual funds; and

(D) evaluate risk and return of various investment options, including stocks, bonds, and mutual funds.

(6) Saving and investing. The student demonstrates an understanding of the importance of planning for retirement. The student is expected to: (Chapters 1, 2, 3, 11)

(A) identify costs of retirement such as living expenses, health care expenses, and long-term care expenses;

(B) identify and explain sources of income during retirement, including Social Security, individual savings, and employer-sponsored plans; and

(C) demonstrate an understanding of the importance of saving early and at a sufficient level to achieve financial security in retirement.

(7) Credit and borrowing. The student understands the use of credit to make purchases. The student is expected to: (Chapter 5)

(A) compare and contrast sources of credit such as banks, merchants, peer-to-peer, payday loans, and title loans;

(B) compare and contrast types of credit, including revolving and installment credit, and collateralized loans versus unsecured credit; and

(C) evaluate the impact of credit decisions on monthly budget, income statement, and net worth statement.

(8) Credit and borrowing. The student identifies factors that affect credit worthiness. The student is expected to: (Various Chapters throughout)

(A) discuss how character, capacity, and collateral can adversely or positively impact an individual's credit rating and the ability to obtain credit;

(B) identify factors that could lead to bankruptcy such as medical expenses, job loss, divorce, or a failed business; and

(C) appraise the impact of borrowing decisions on credit score, including consequences of poor credit management and bankruptcy.

(9) Credit and borrowing. The student evaluates a decision to use credit. The student is expected to: (Chapter 5, 10)

(A) examine the components of the cost of borrowing, including annual percentage rate (APR), fixed versus variable interest, length of term, grace period, and additional fees such as late payment, cash advance, and prepayment penalties;

(B) explain strategies to reduce total cost of borrowing such as making a higher down payment and additional principal payments; and

(C) differentiate between the use and cost of debit and credit cards.

(10) Insuring and protecting. The student recognizes financial risks faced by individuals and families and identifies strategies for handling these risks. The student is expected to: (Various Chapters throughout)

(A) identify risk as potential loss of assets or earning potential; and

(B) apply risk management strategies, including avoiding, reducing, retaining, and transferring risk.

(11) Insuring and protecting. The student identifies the costs and benefits of insurance for transferring risk. The student is expected to: (Chapter 9, 10, 11)

(A) define insurance terminology, including premiums, deductibles, co-pays, and policy limits;

(B) explain the costs and benefits of different types and sources of health insurance such as individual health plans, employer-provided health plans, and government-provided health plans;

(C) explain the costs and benefits of disability and long-term care insurance;

(D) explain the costs and benefits of life insurance, including term insurance and whole life insurance;

(E) explain the costs and benefits of property insurance, including homeowner's and renter's insurance;

(F) explain the costs and benefits of automobile insurance and factors that impact the price of insurance, including the type of vehicle, age and sex of driver, driving record, deductible, and geographic location; and

(12) Insuring and protecting. The student understands the legal instruments available for estate planning. The student is expected to: (Chapter 11)

    (A) explain the importance of guardianship of minor children, wills, and beneficiary designation;

(13) College and postsecondary education and training. The student recognizes the costs and benefits of various types of college, postsecondary education, and training. The student is expected to: (Chapter 8)

    (A) analyze the relationship between education and training and earnings;

    (B) identify types of costs associated with college, postsecondary education, and training;

    (C) compare costs among postsecondary education and training institutions such as public universities, private universities, certification programs, and community colleges; and

    (D) analyze the quality of education investment using measures such as academic reputation, selectivity and rigor in a chosen area of study, average starting salary of students graduating in chosen field, and likelihood of student graduation.

(14) College and postsecondary education and training. The student understands various options for paying for college, postsecondary education, and training. The student is expected to: (Chapter 8)

    (A) understand how, why, and when to complete grant and scholarship applications and the Free Application for Federal Student Aid (FAFSA) provided by the U.S. Department of Education;

    (B) research various sources of funds for postsecondary education and training, including student loans, grants and scholarships, and other sources such as work-study and military programs; and

    (C) analyze the advantages and disadvantages of various sources of funds for postsecondary education and training, including student loans, grants and scholarships, and other sources such as work-study and military programs.

Mathematical Models with Applications

(1) Mathematical modeling in personal finance. The student uses mathematical processes with graphical and numerical techniques to study patterns and analyze data related to personal finance. The student is expected to:

    (A) use rates and linear functions to solve problems involving personal finance and budgeting, including compensations and deductions; (Chapter 4)

    (B) solve problems involving personal taxes; (Chapter 7) and

    (C) analyze data to make decisions about banking, including options for online banking, checking accounts, overdraft protection, processing fees, and debit card/ATM fees. (Chapter 5)

(2) Mathematical modeling in personal finance. The student uses mathematical processes with algebraic formulas, graphs, and amortization modeling to solve problems involving credit. The student is expected to:

    (A) use formulas to generate tables to display series of payments for loan amortizations resulting from financed purchases; (Chapter 5)

    (B) analyze personal credit options in retail purchasing and compare relative advantages and disadvantages of each option; (Chapter 5)

    (C) use technology to create amortization models to investigate home financing and compare buying a home to renting a home; (Chapter 10)

    (D) use technology to create amortization models to investigate automobile financing and compare buying a vehicle to leasing a vehicle.(Chapter 9)

(3) Mathematical modeling in personal finance. The student uses mathematical processes with algebraic formulas, numerical techniques, and graphs to solve problems related to financial planning. The student is expected to:

    (A) analyze and compare coverage options and rates in insurance; (Chapter 11)

    (B) investigate and compare investment options, including stocks, bonds, annuities, certificates of deposit, and retirement plans; and (Chapters 2, 3)

    (C) analyze types of savings options involving simple and compound interest and compare relative advantages of these options. (Chapter 1)

Made in United States
Troutdale, OR
11/08/2023

14405701R20077